FIRST 50
JAZZ CLASSICS
YOU SHOULD PLAY ON PIANO

ISBN 978-1-70513-147-3

Visit Hal Leonard Online at
www.halleonard.com

Contact Us:
Hal Leonard
7777 West Bluemound Road
Milwaukee, WI 53213
Email: info@halleonard.com

In Europe, contact:
Hal Leonard Europe Limited
42 Wigmore Street
Marylebone, London, W1U 2RN
Email: info@halleonardeurope.com

In Australia, contact:
Hal Leonard Australia Pty. Ltd.
4 Lentara Court
Cheltenham, Victoria, 3192 Australia
Email: info@halleonard.com.au

CONTENTS

7 . . . . Afternoon in Paris

4 . . . . All Blues

10 . . . . Angel Eyes

13 . . . . As Time Goes By

16 . . . . Birdland

22 . . . . Bluesette

27 . . . . Bye Bye Blackbird

30 . . . . Caravan

34 . . . . A Child Is Born

36 . . . . Desafinado

41 . . . . Do Nothin' Till You Hear from Me

44 . . . . Doxy

52 . . . . Easy to Love (You'd Be So Easy to Love)

54 . . . . Embraceable You

58 . . . . Emily

62 . . . . Estate

47 . . . . Fascinating Rhythm

66 . . . . Footprints

68 . . . . Four

70 . . . . Gentle Rain

76 . . . . Good Bait

82 . . . . Goodbye Pork Pie Hat

73 . . . . Have You Met Miss Jones?

79 . . . . Honeysuckle Rose

84 . . . . I Remember You

91 . . . . I'm Getting Sentimental Over You

94 . . . . In Walked Bud

96 . . . . In Your Own Sweet Way

88 . . . . Killer Joe

98 . . . . Little Sunflower

101 . . . . Lullaby of Birdland

104 . . . . Mercy, Mercy, Mercy

106 . . . . My Foolish Heart

112 . . . . Naima (Niema)

114 . . . . Night Train

109 . . . . Nuages

118 . . . . On Green Dolphin Street

122 . . . . Recorda Me

127 . . . . St. Thomas

130 . . . . The Shadow of Your Smile

134 . . . . Sidewinder

136 . . . . Stompin' at the Savoy

138 . . . . Take Five

124 . . . . Take the "A" Train

145 . . . . The Very Thought of You

142 . . . . Watch What Happens

148 . . . . Willow Weep for Me

154 . . . . Witchcraft

151 . . . . Yardbird Suite

158 . . . . Yesterdays

ALL BLUES

By MILES DAVIS

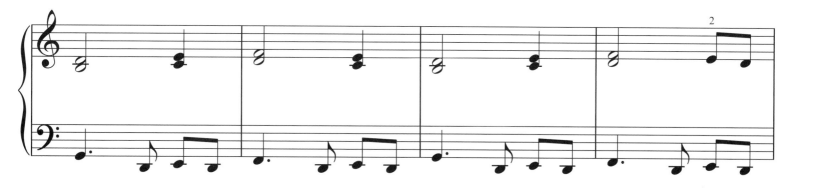

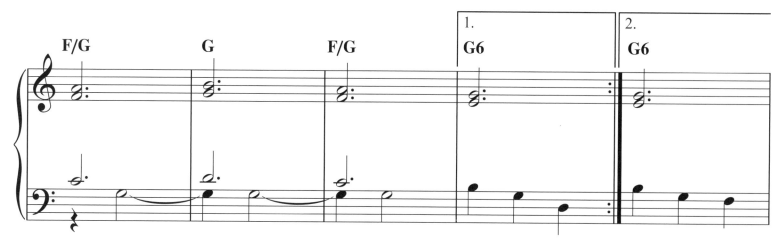

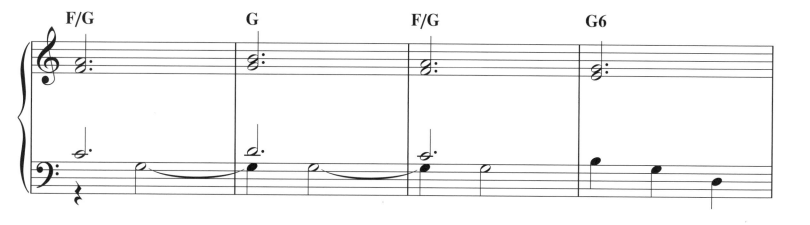

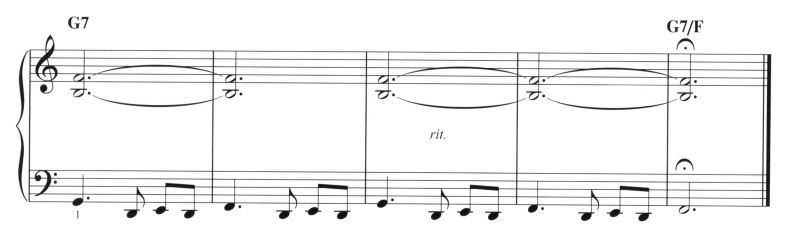

AFTERNOON IN PARIS

By JOHN LEWIS

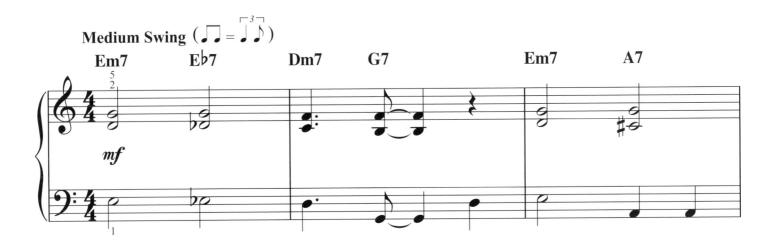

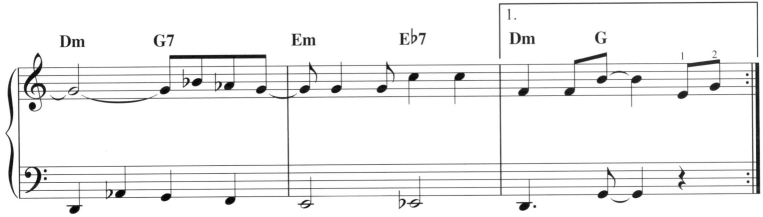

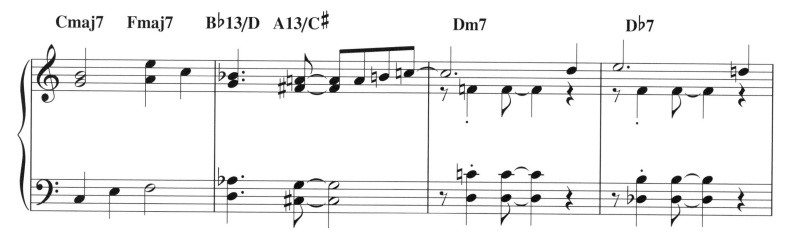

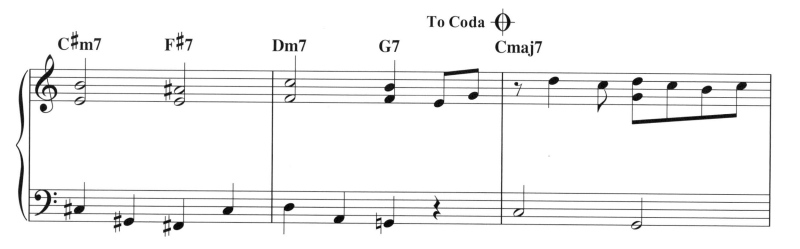

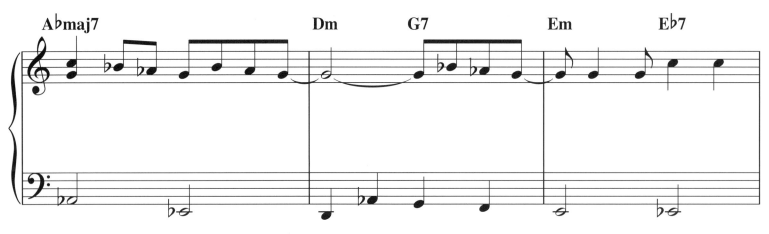

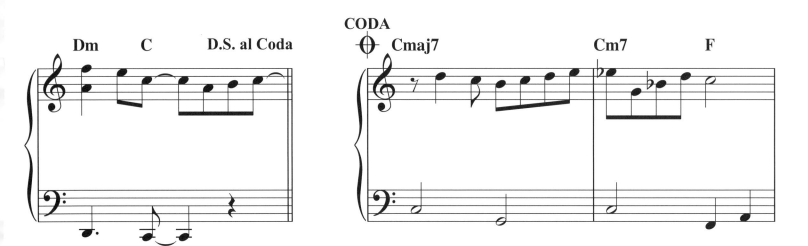

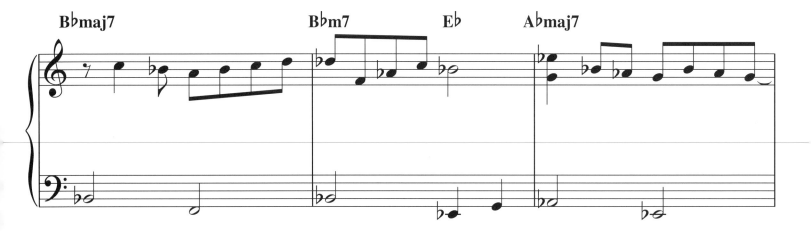

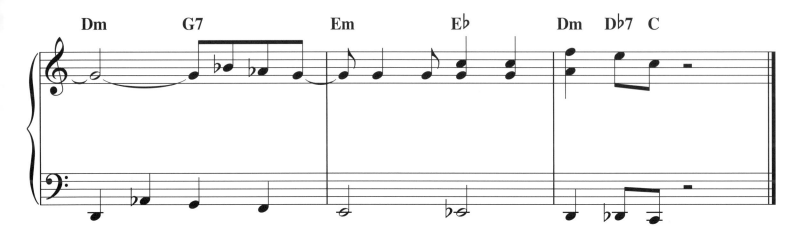

ANGEL EYES

Words by EARL BRENT
Music by MATT DENNIS

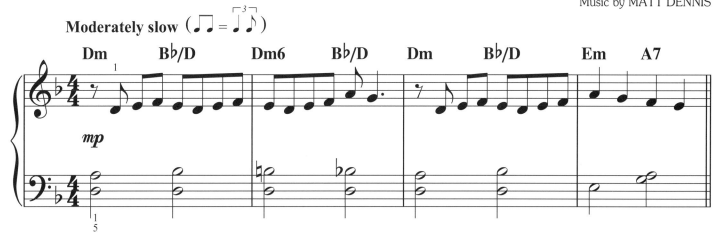

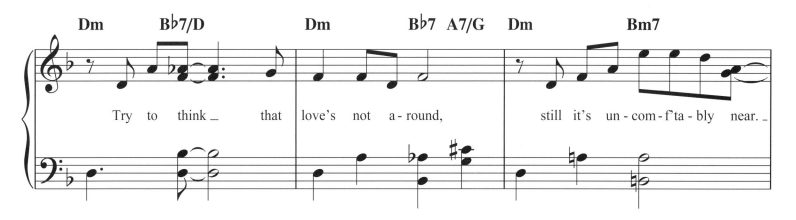

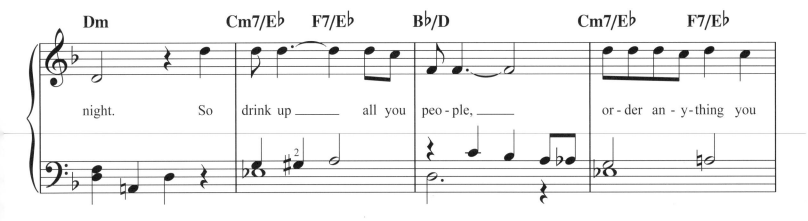

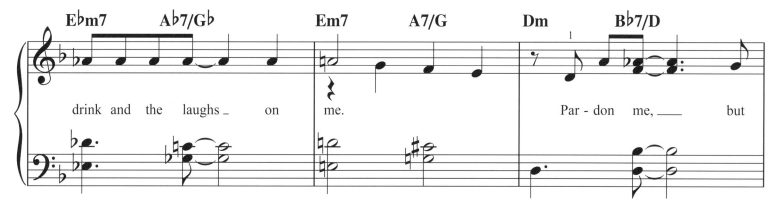

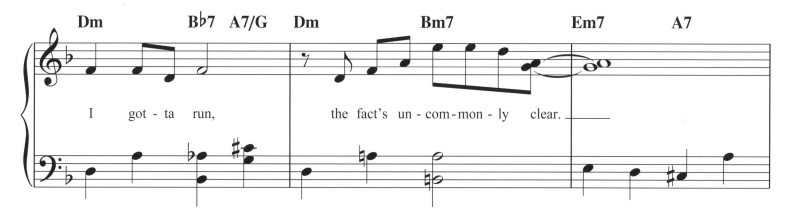

AS TIME GOES BY

from CASABLANCA

Words and Music by
HERMAN HUPFELD

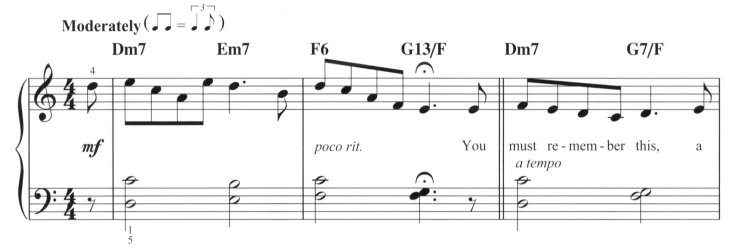

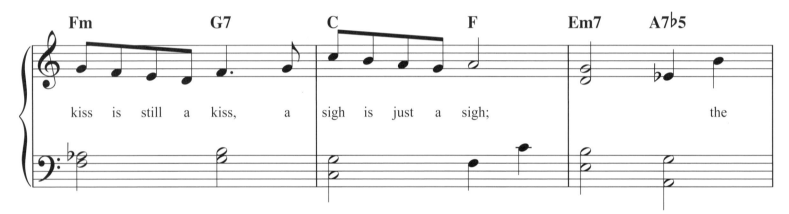

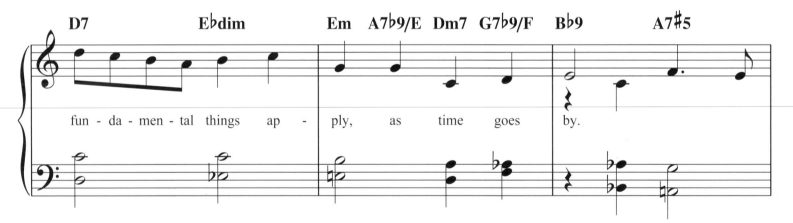

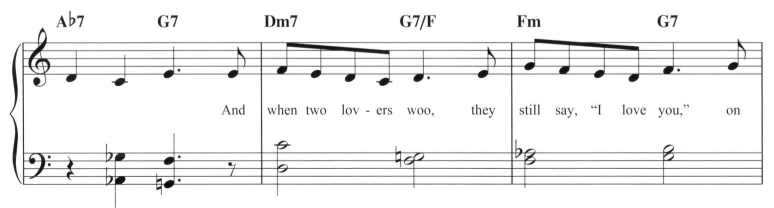

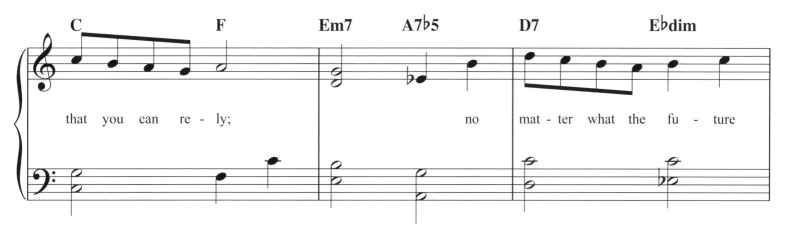

that you can re - ly;   no mat - ter what the fu - ture

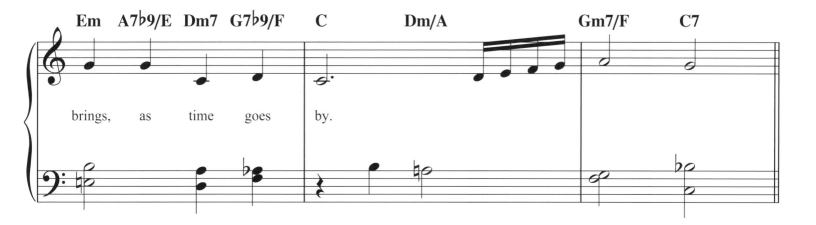

brings,   as   time   goes   by.

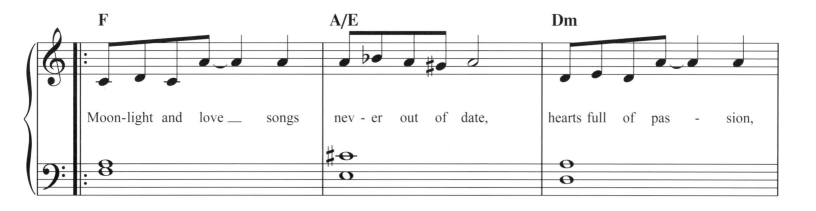

Moon-light and love __ songs   nev - er out of date,   hearts full of pas - sion,

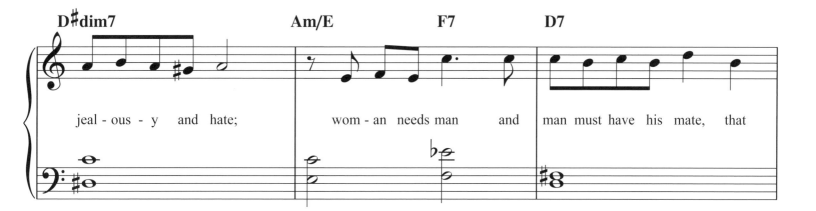

jeal - ous - y and hate;   wom - an needs man   and   man must have his mate,   that

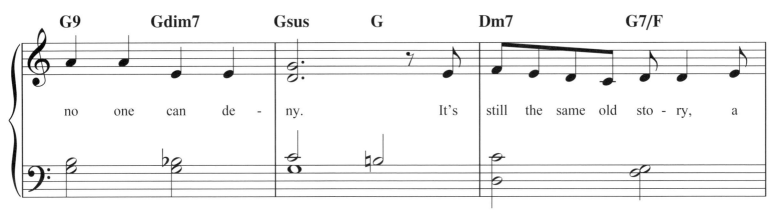

no one can de - ny. It's still the same old sto - ry, a

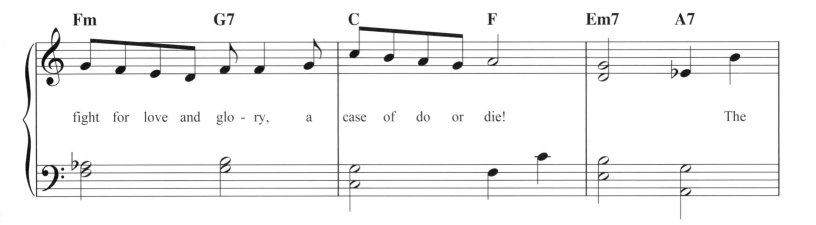

fight for love and glo - ry, a case of do or die! The

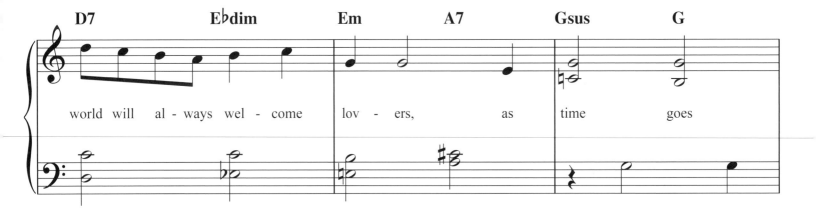

world will al - ways wel - come lov - ers, as time goes

by.

by.

BIRDLAND

Words by JON HENDRICKS
Music by JOSEF ZAWINUL

Moderately fast

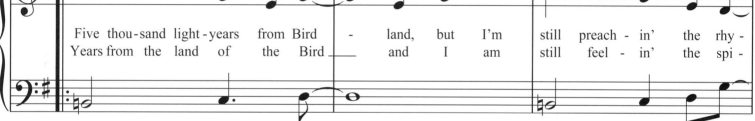

Five thou-sand light-years from Bird - land, but I'm still preach-in' the rhy-
Years from the land of the Bird and I am still feel-in' the spi-

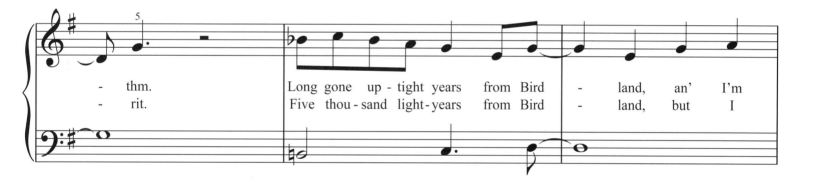

- thm.
Long gone up-tight years from Bird - land, an' I'm
- rit.
Five thou-sand light-years from Bird - land, but I

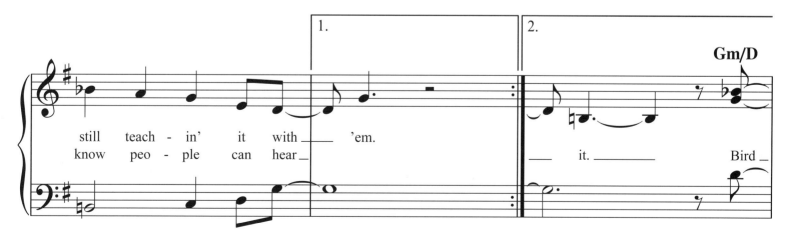

still teach-in' it with 'em.
know peo-ple can hear it.

Gm/D

it. Bird

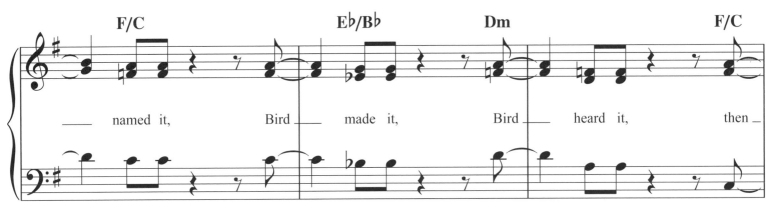

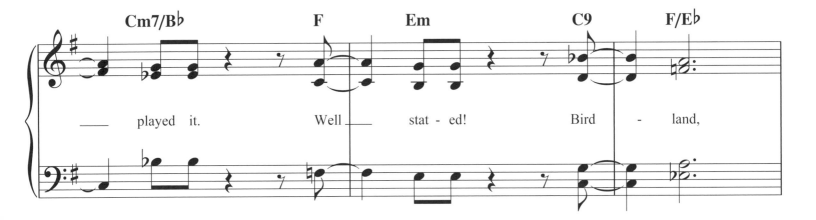

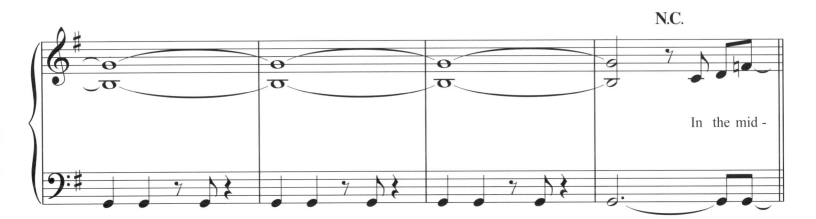

18

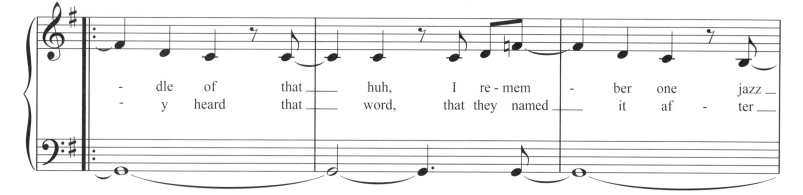

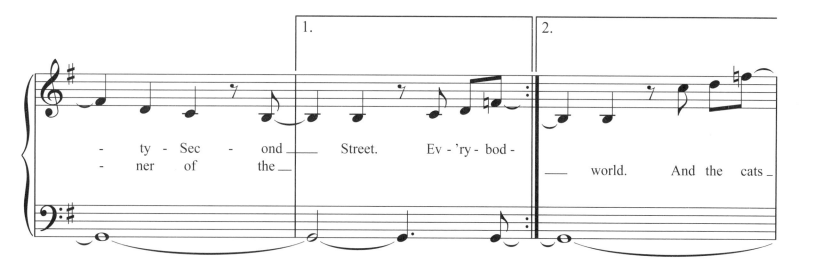

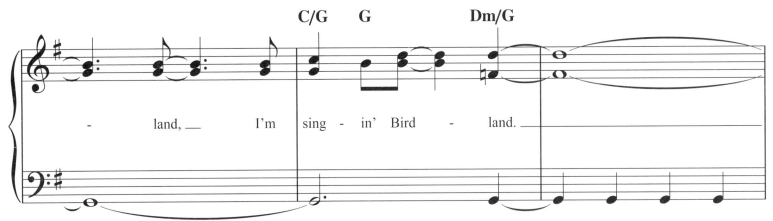

- land, __ I'm sing - in' Bird - land. __

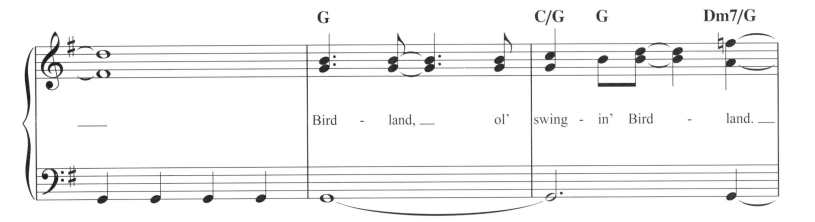

__ Bird - land, __ ol' swing - in' Bird - land. __

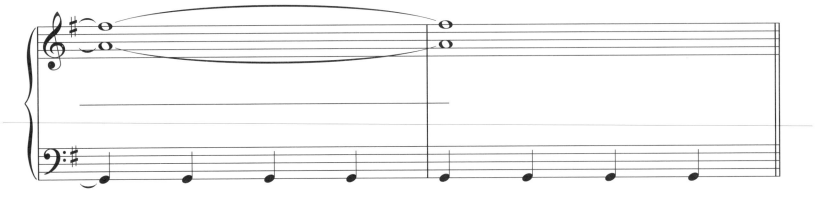

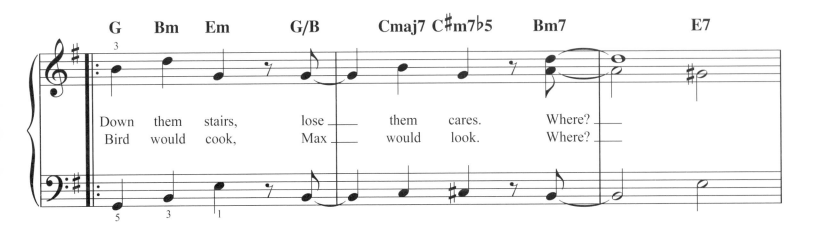

Down them stairs, lose __ them cares. Where? __
Bird would cook, Max __ would look. Where? __

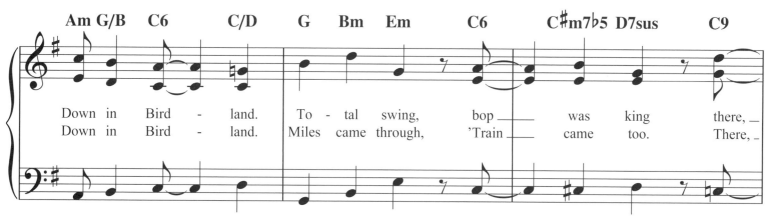

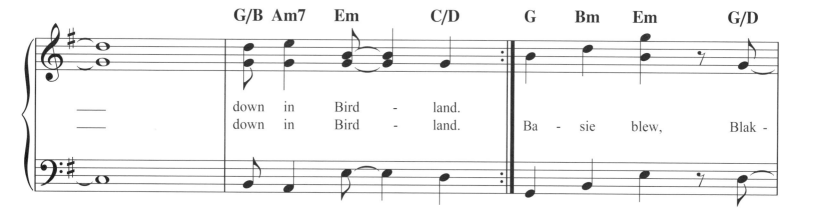

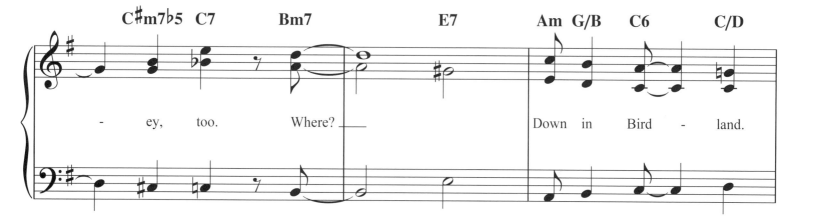

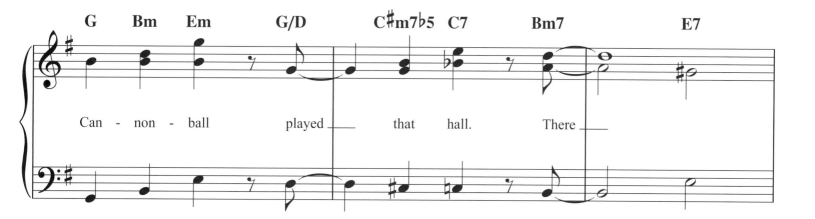

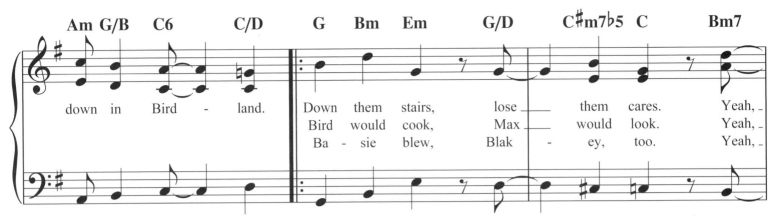

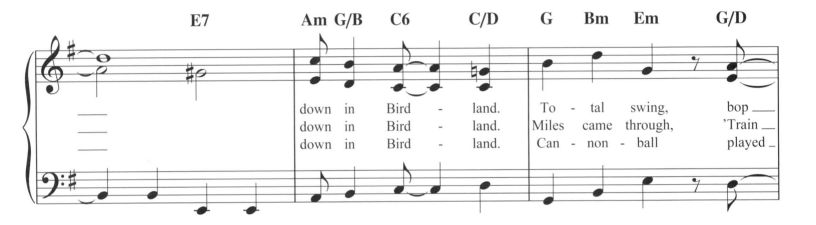

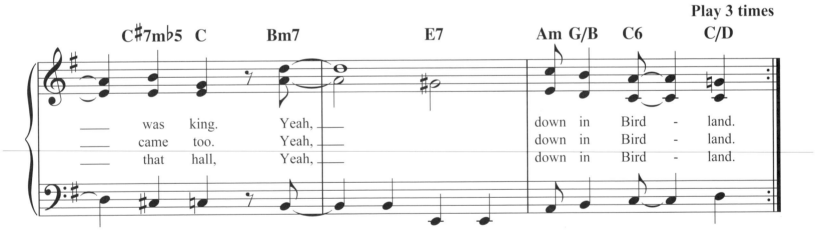

Play 3 times

BLUESETTE

Words by NORMAN GIMBEL
Music by JEAN THIELEMANS

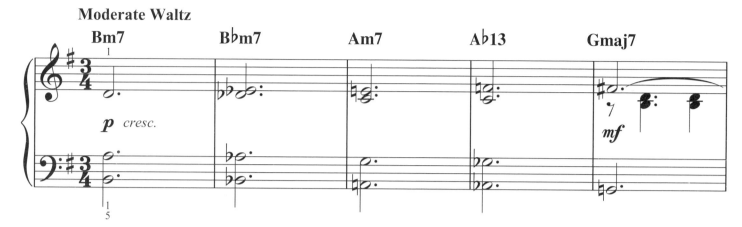

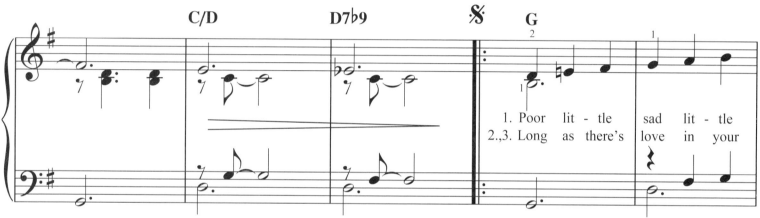

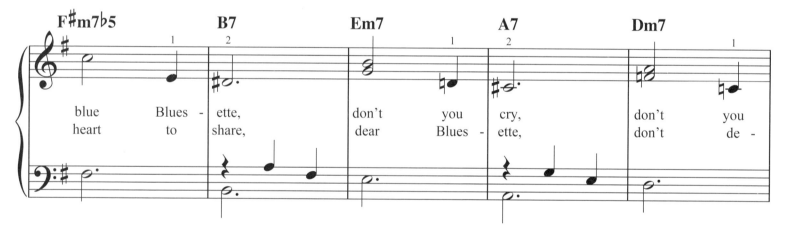

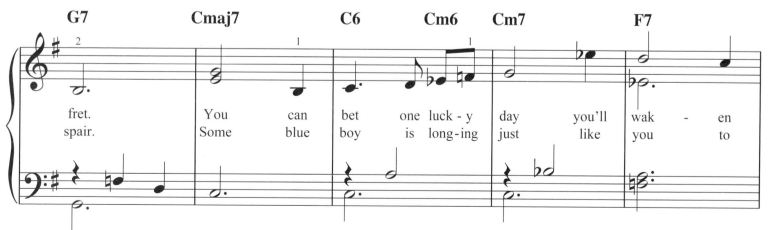

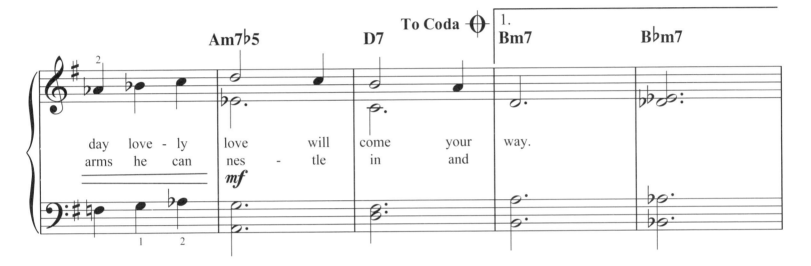

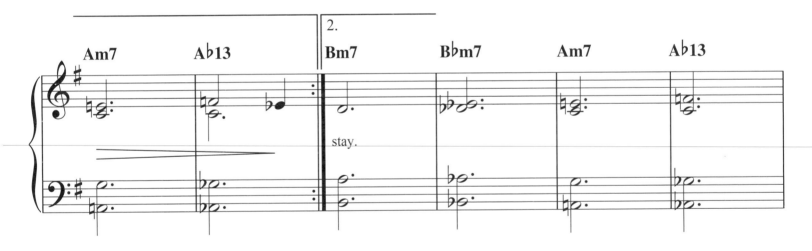

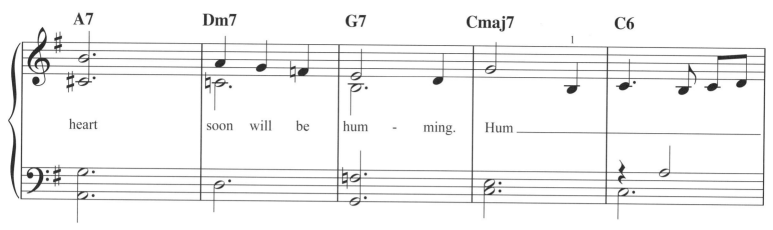

heart   soon will be   hum - ming.   Hum _____

_____   Doo - ya, doo - ya, doo - ya,   doo - ya, doo - ya, doo - ya,   doo - oo -

oo,   Blues - ette.

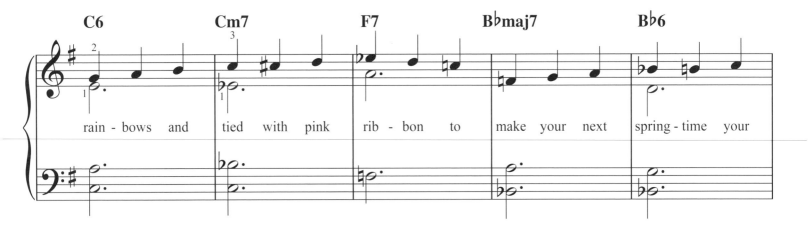

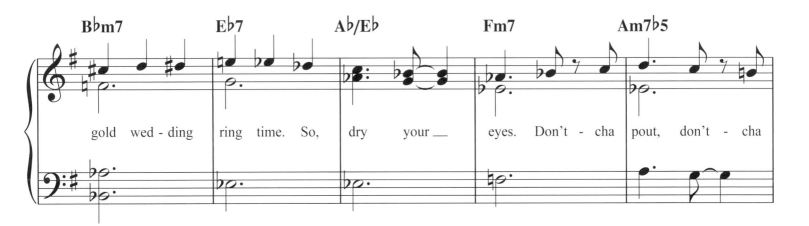

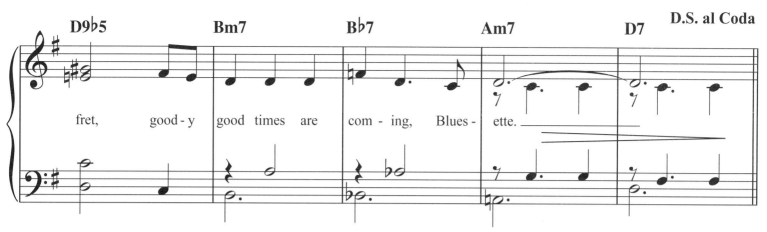

D.S. al Coda

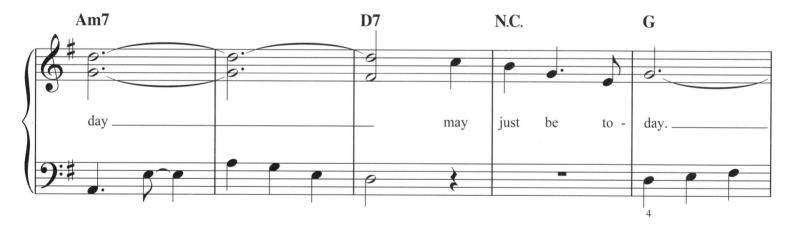

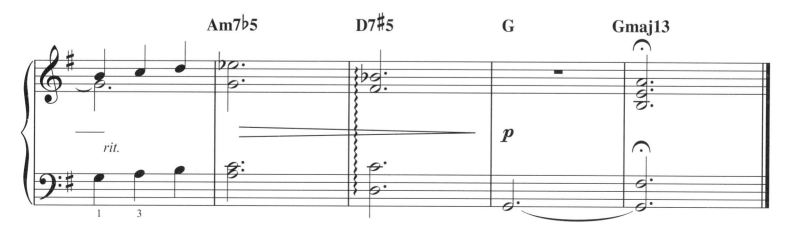

BYE BYE BLACKBIRD

from PETE KELLY'S BLUES

Words by MORT DIXON
Music by RAY HENDERSON

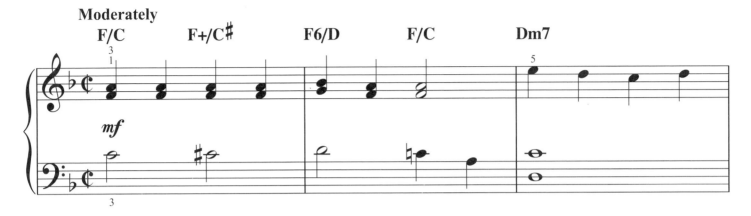

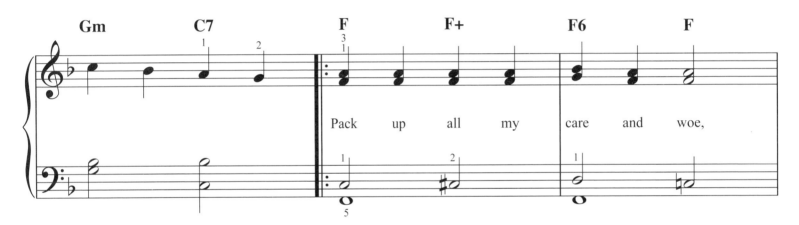

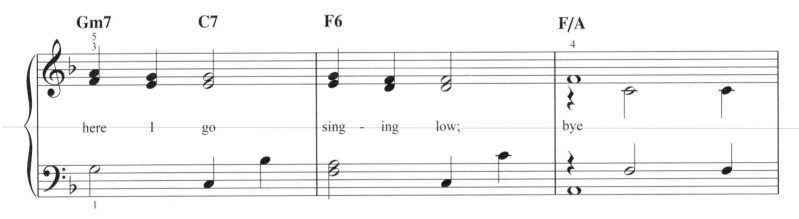

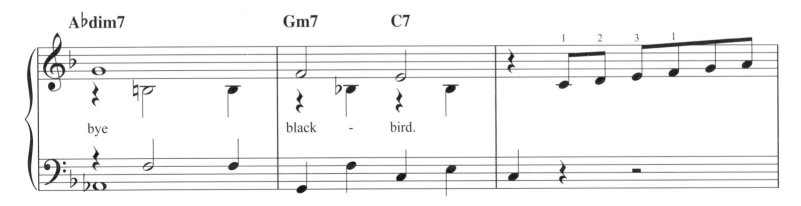

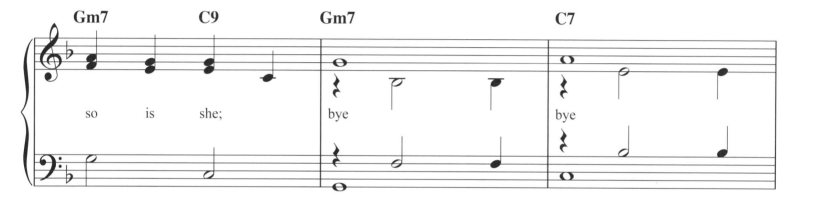

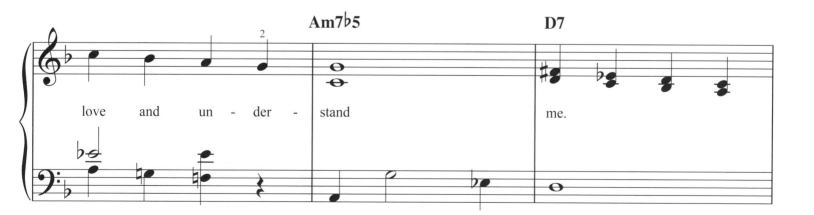

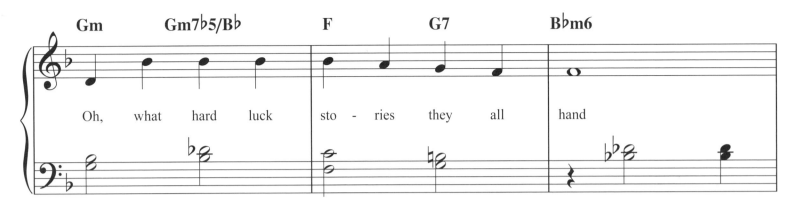

Oh, what hard luck sto - ries they all hand

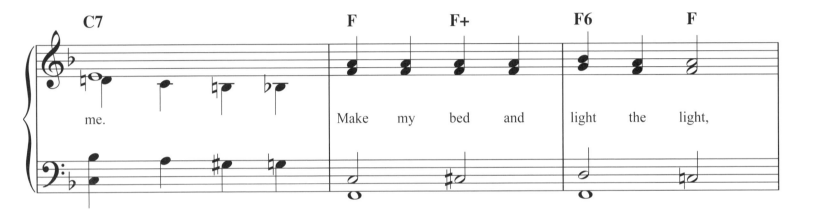

me. Make my bed and light the light,

I'll ar - rive late to - night; black - bird _____ bye

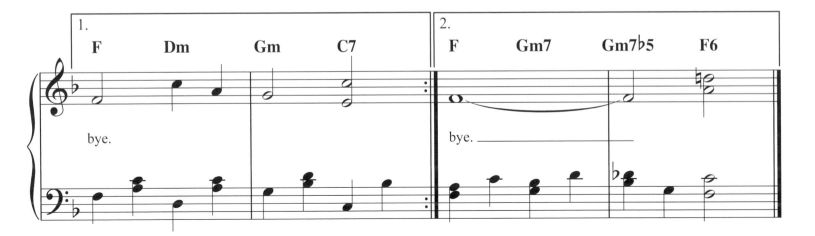

bye.   bye. _____

CARAVAN

Words and Music by DUKE ELLINGTON,
IRVING MILLS and JUAN TIZOL

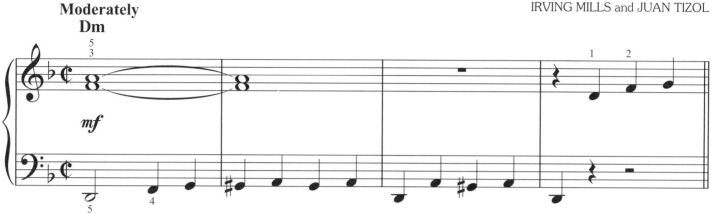

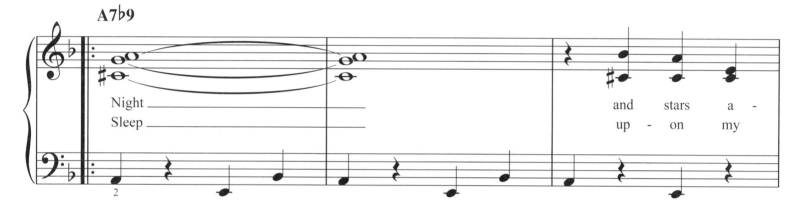

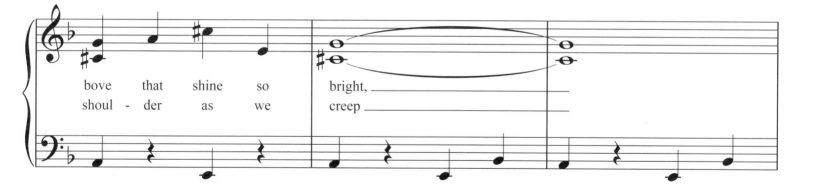

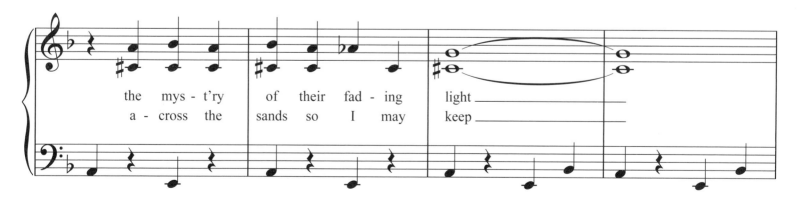

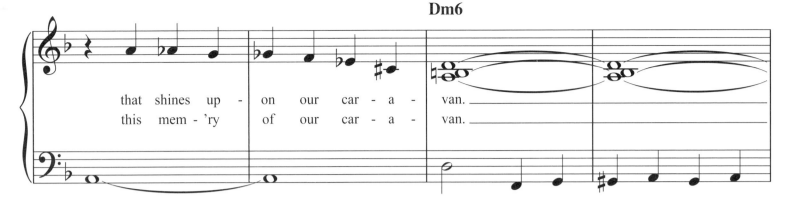

Dm6

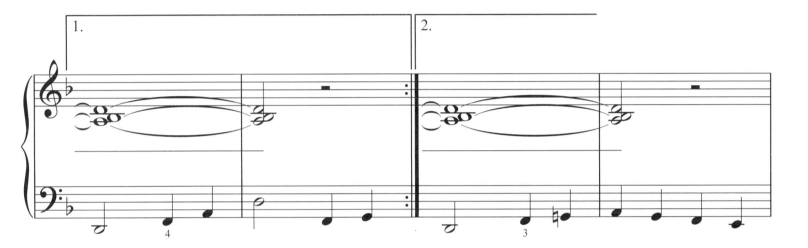

that shines up - on our car - a - van. _____
this mem - 'ry of our car - a - van. _____

1.   2.

D7

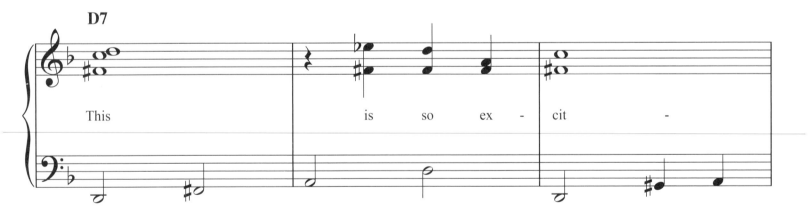

This   is so ex - cit -

D+   **G7**

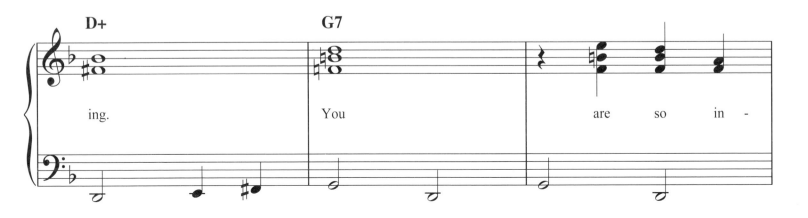

ing.   You   are so in -

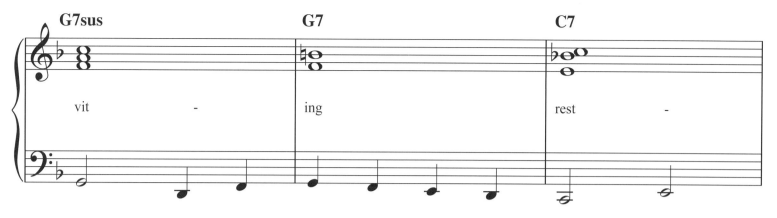

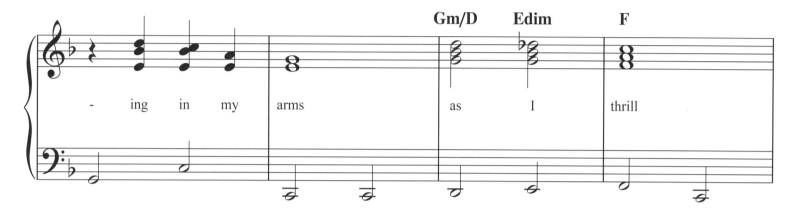

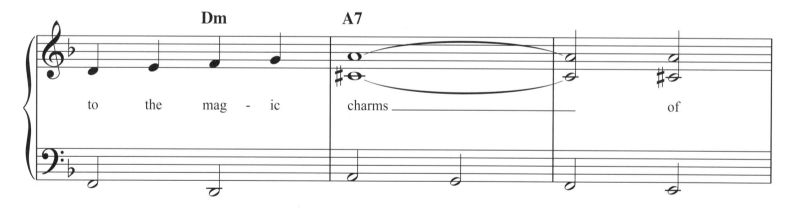

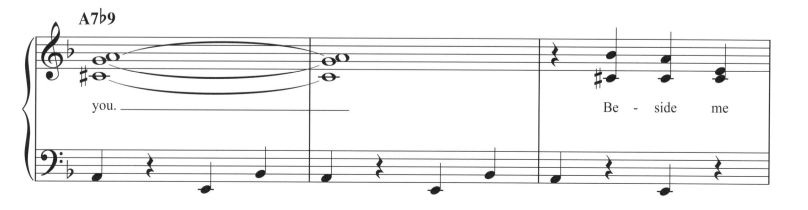

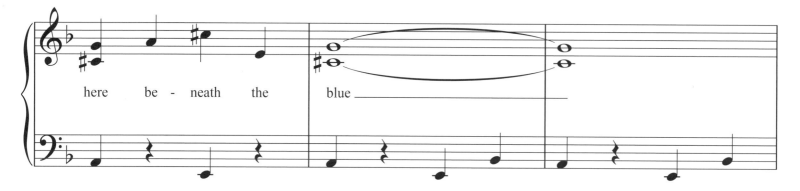

here be - neath the blue _____

my dream of love is com - ing true _____

_____ with - in our des - ert car - a -

Dm6

van. _____

A CHILD IS BORN

Music by THAD JONES
Lyrics by ALEC WILDER

Slow Jazz Ballad

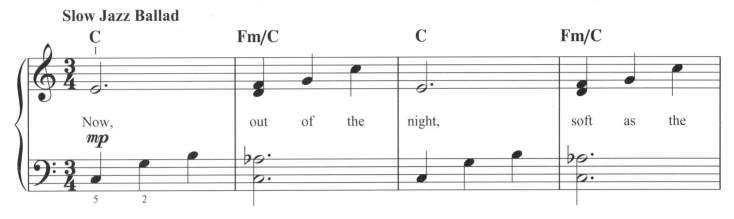

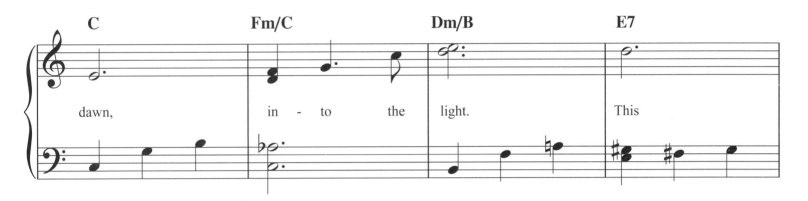

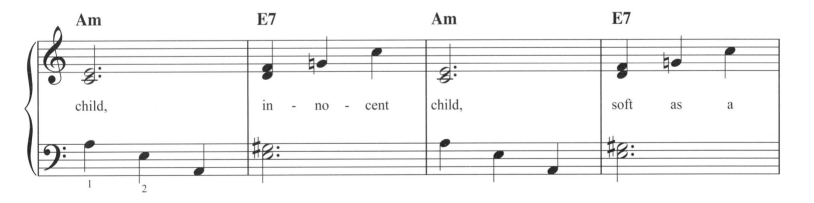

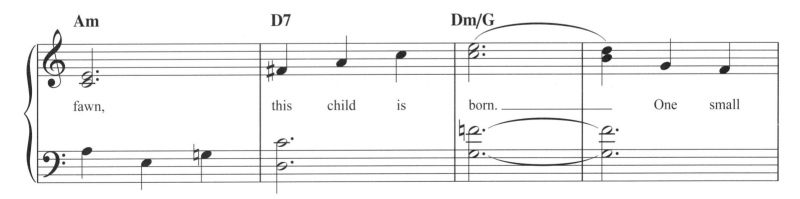

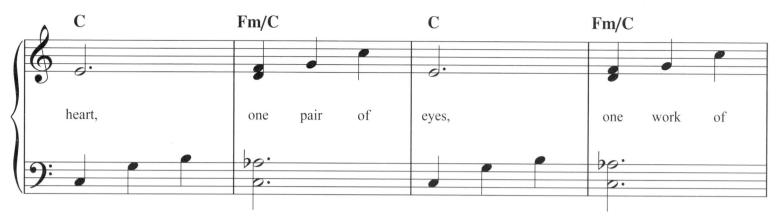

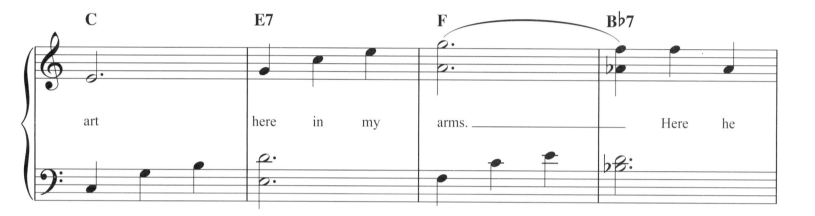

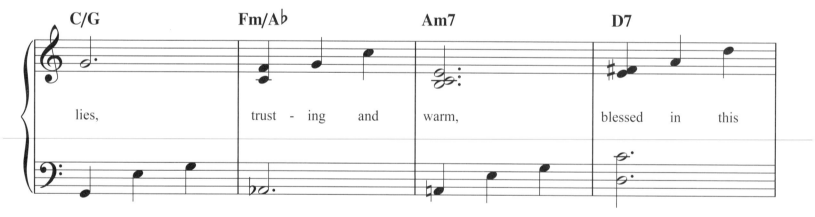

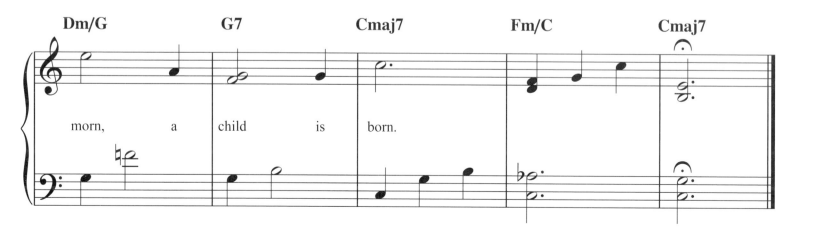

DESAFINADO

Original Text by NEWTON MENDONÇA
Music by ANTONIO CARLOS JOBIM

Easy Bossa Nova

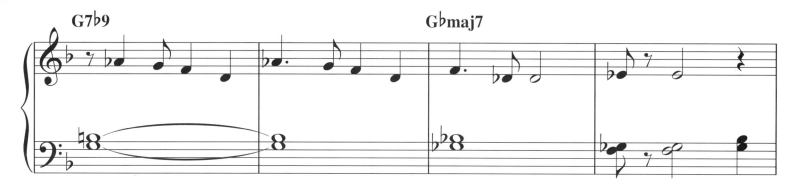

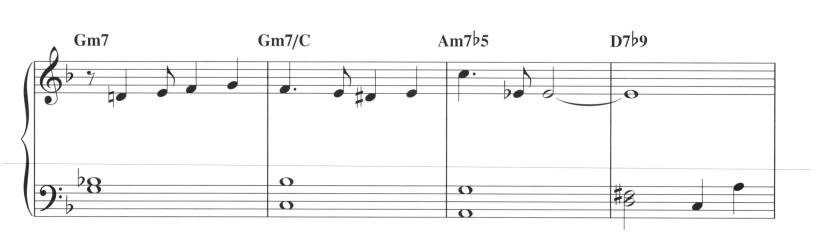

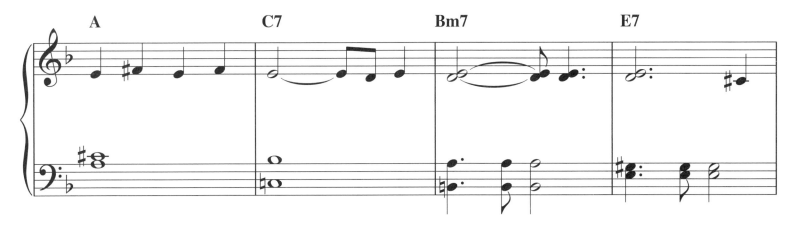

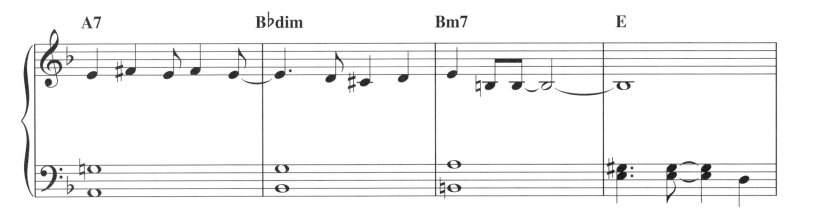

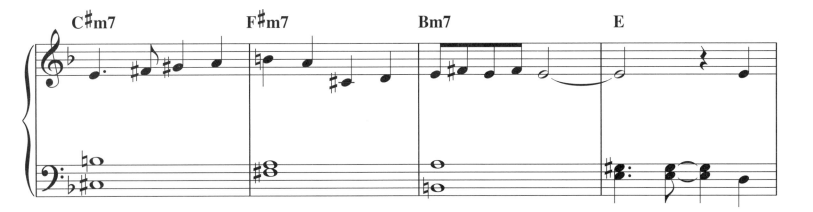

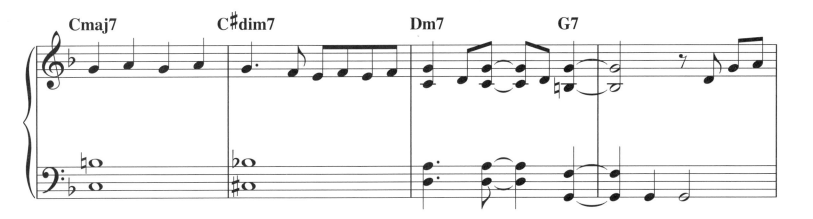

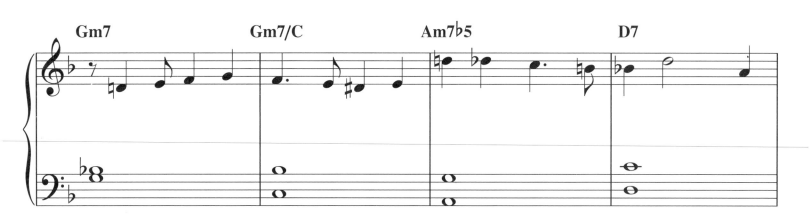

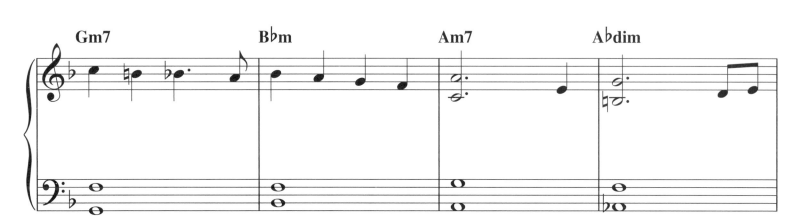

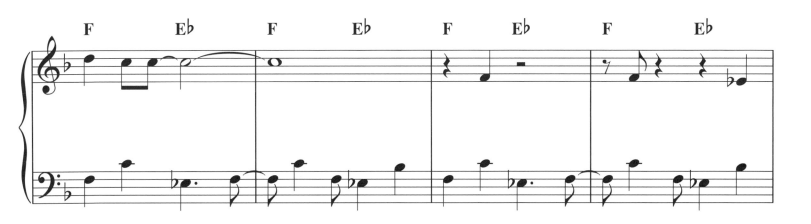

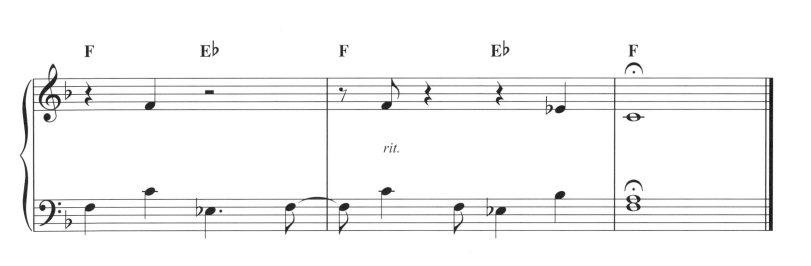

DO NOTHIN' TILL YOU HEAR FROM ME

Words and Music by DUKE ELLINGTON
and BOB RUSSELL

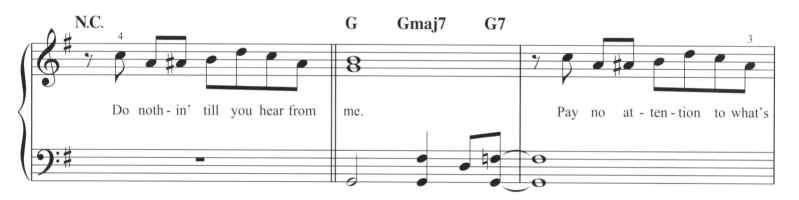

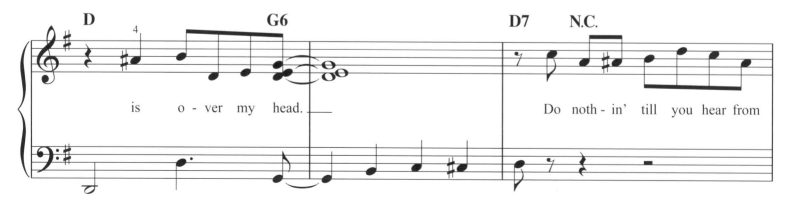

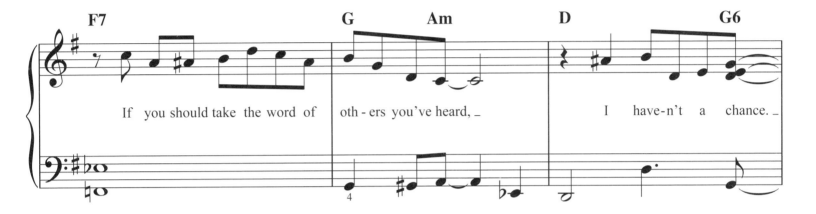

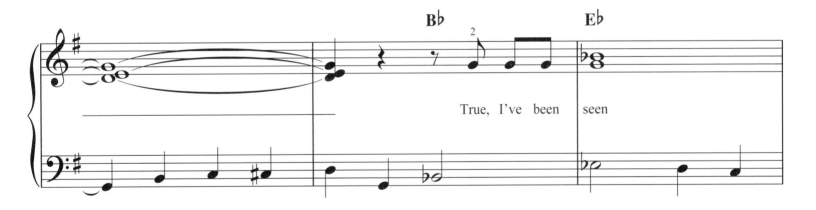

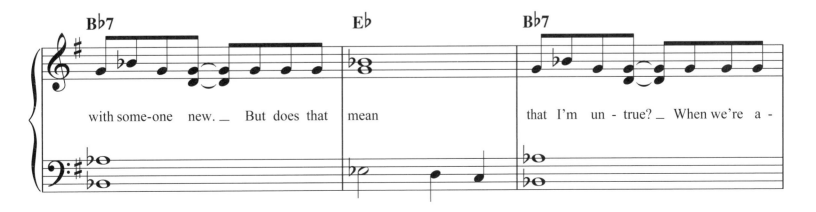

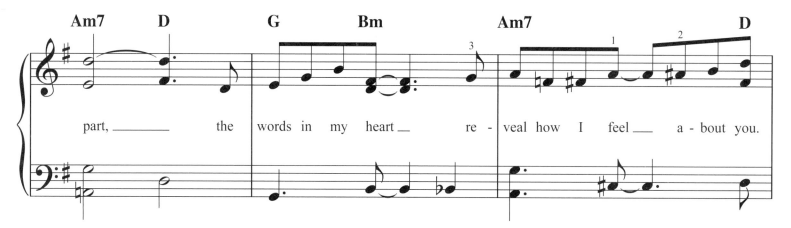

part, _____ the words in my heart __ re - veal how I feel __ a - bout you.

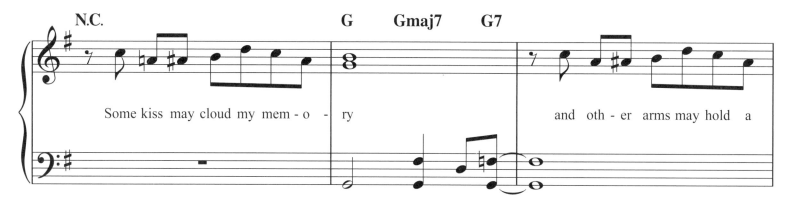

Some kiss may cloud my mem - o - ry and oth - er arms may hold a

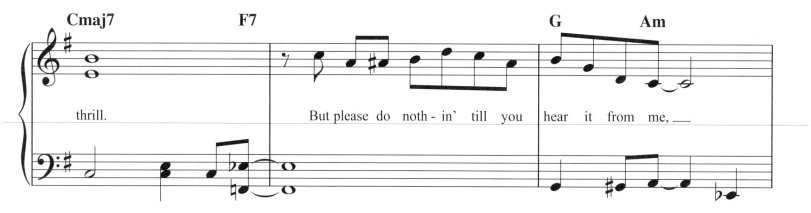

thrill. But please do noth - in' till you hear it from me, __

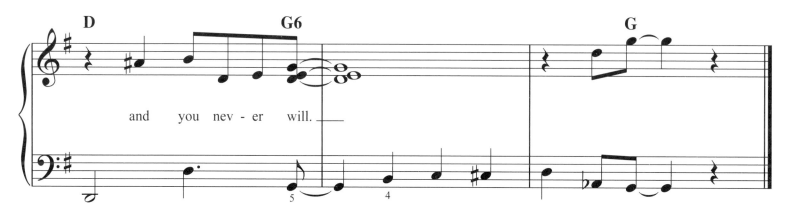

and you nev - er will. __

DOXY

By SONNY ROLLINS

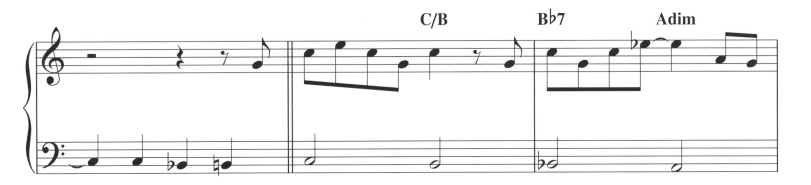

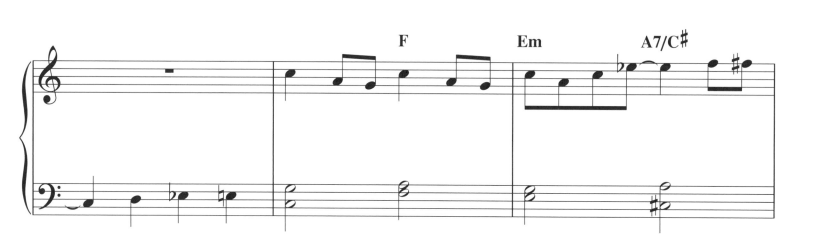

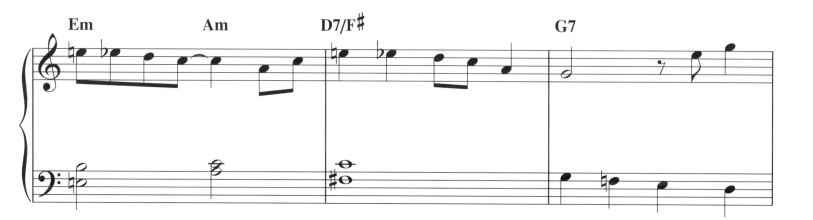

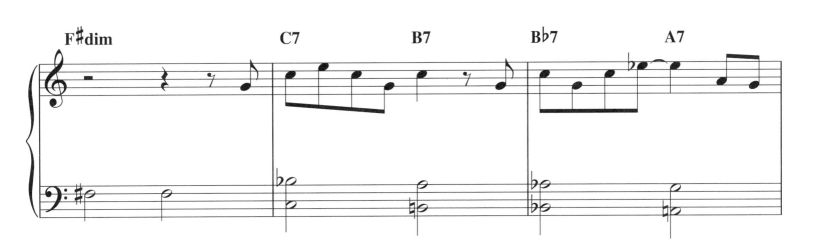

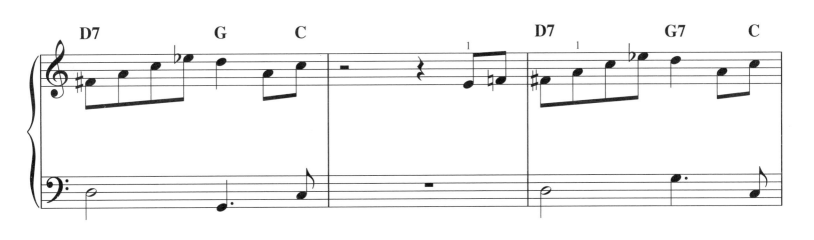

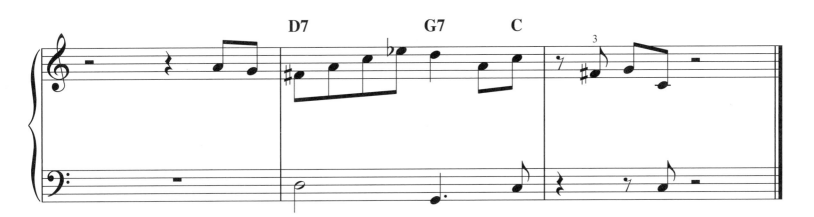

FASCINATING RHYTHM

from the Broadway Musical LADY, BE GOOD

Music and Lyrics by GEORGE GERSHWIN
and IRA GERSHWIN

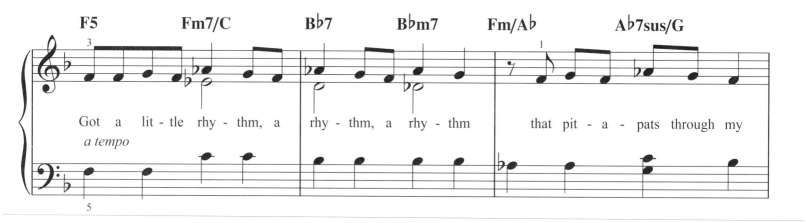

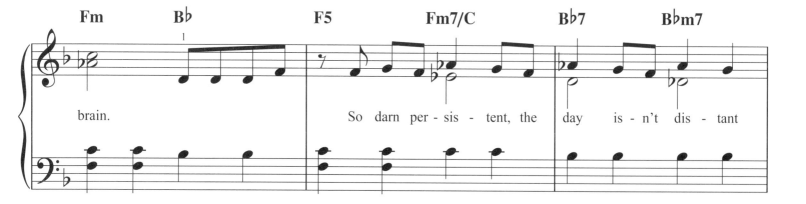

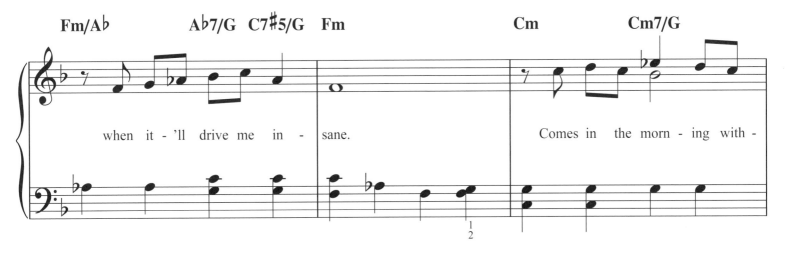

when it - 'll drive me in - sane.   Comes in the morn - ing with -

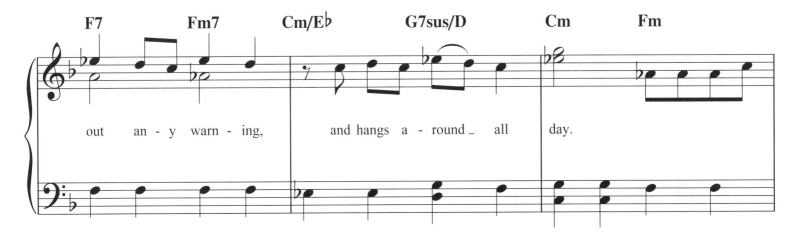

out an - y warn - ing,   and hangs a - round _ all   day.

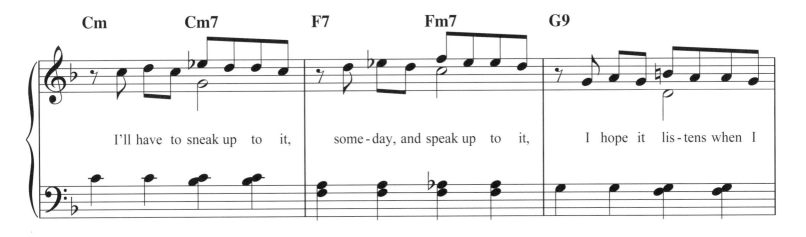

I'll have to sneak up to it,   some - day, and speak up to it,   I hope it lis - tens when I

say: Fas - ci - nat - ing rhy - thm you've got me on the go!   Fas - ci -

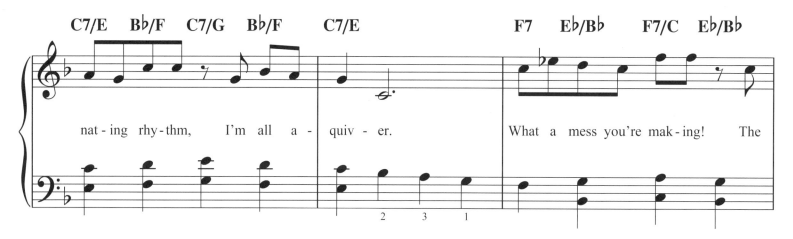

nat - ing rhy - thm, I'm all a - quiv - er. What a mess you're mak - ing! The

neigh - bors want to know why I'm al - ways shak - ing just like a

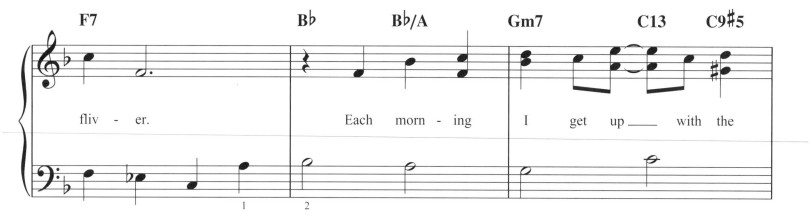

fliv - er. Each morn - ing I get up ___ with the

sun, (start a - hop - ping nev - er stop - ping) to find at

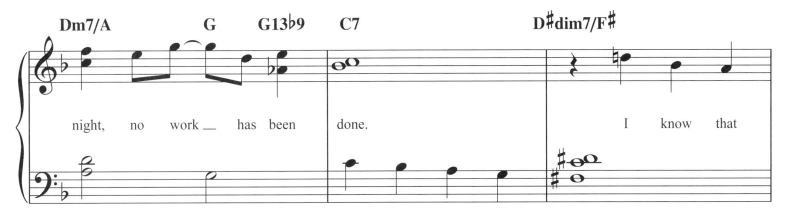

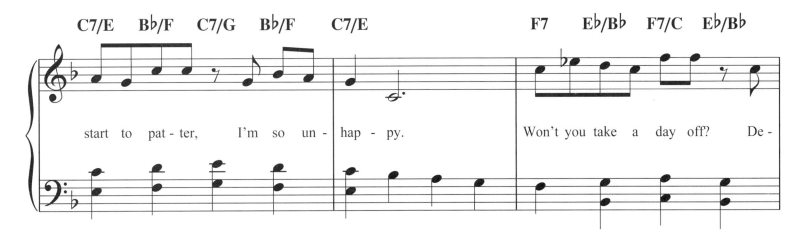

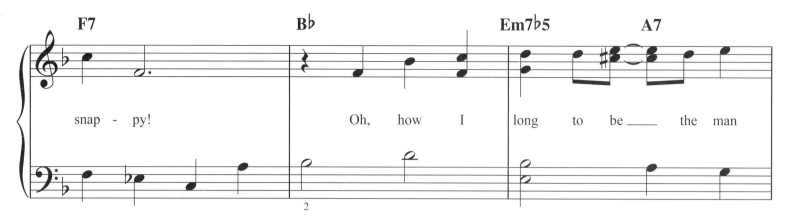

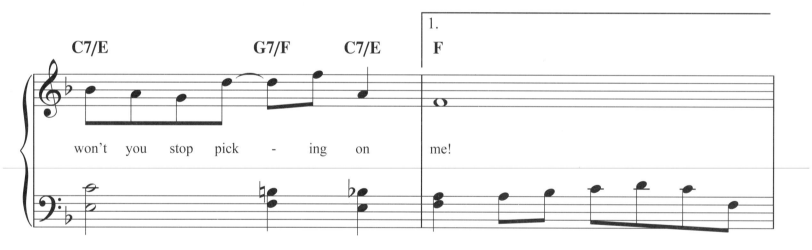

EASY TO LOVE
(You'd Be So Easy to Love)

Words and Music by
COLE PORTER

Slowly, with expression

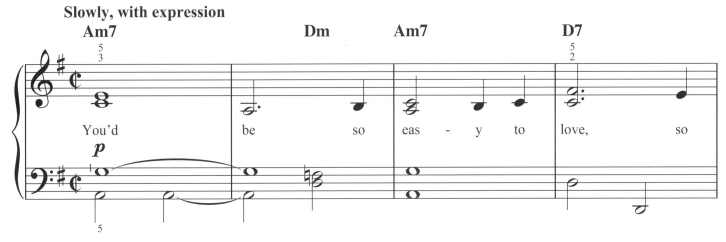

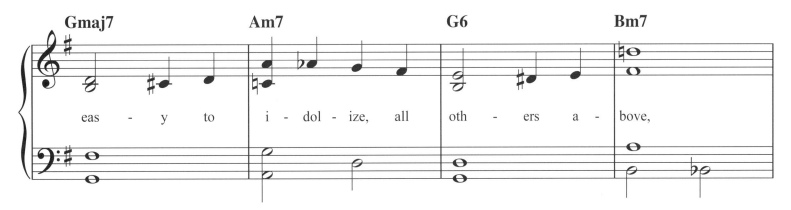

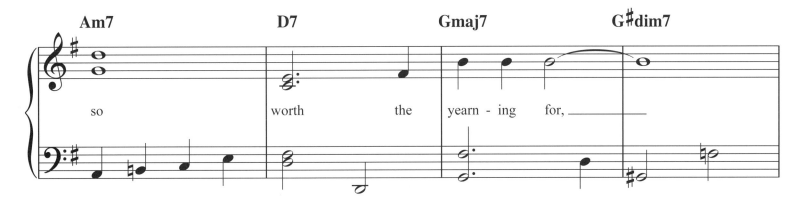

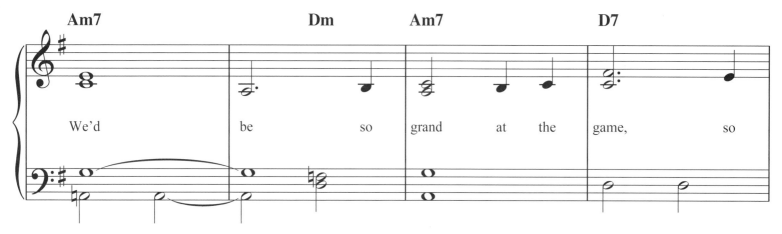

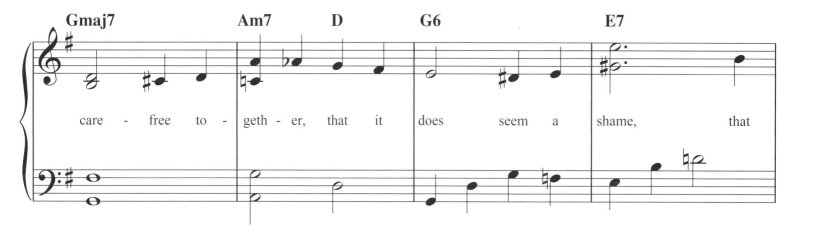

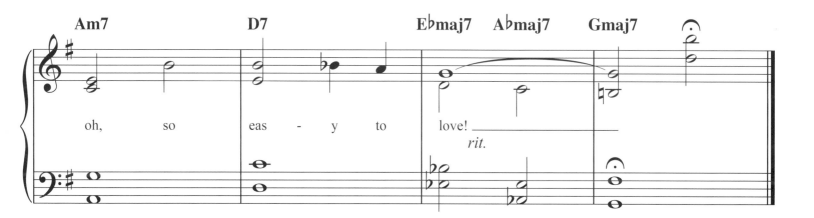

EMBRACEABLE YOU

from GIRL CRAZY

Music and Lyrics by GEORGE GERSHWIN
and IRA GERSHWIN

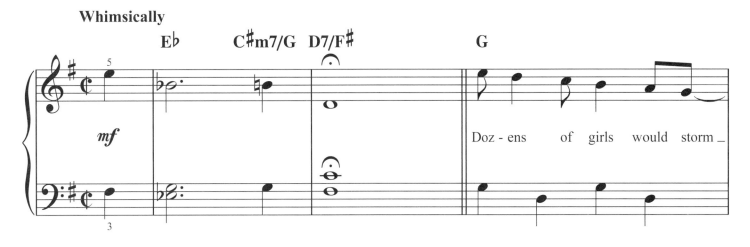

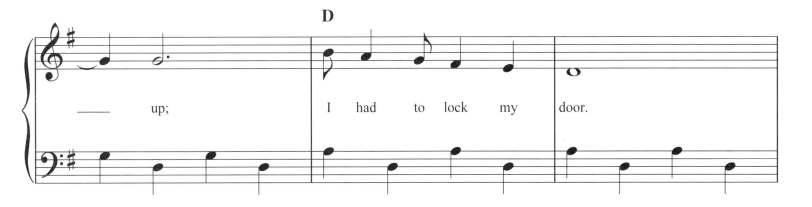

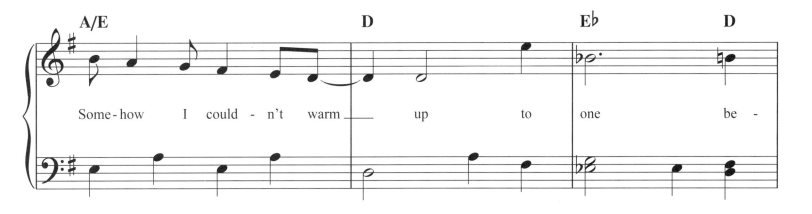

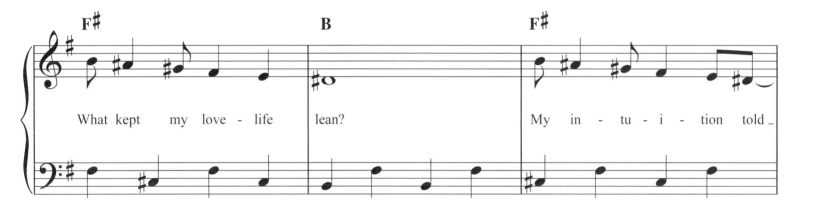

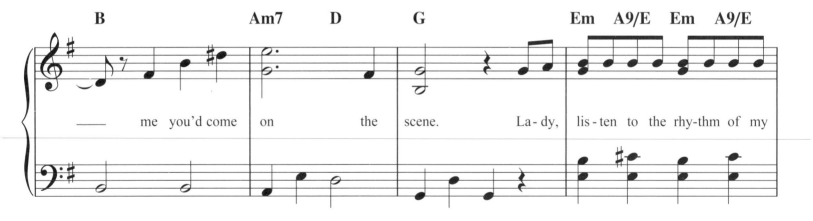

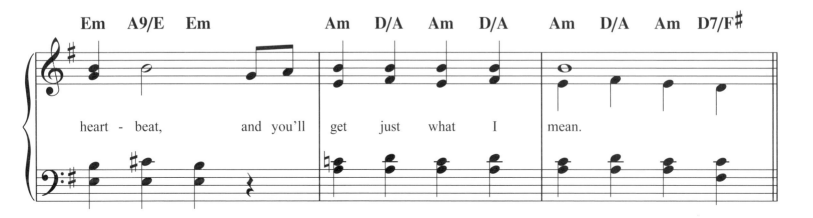

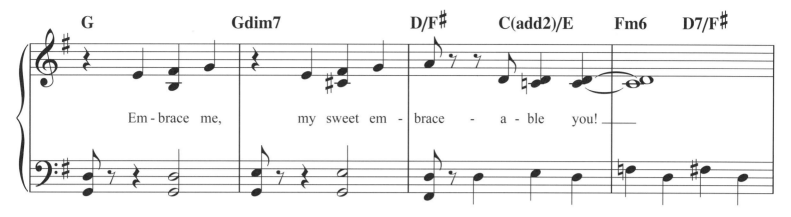

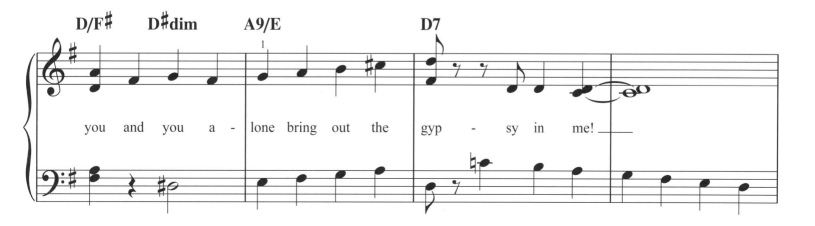

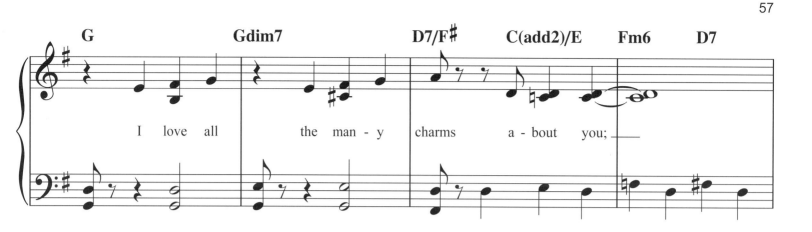

I love all the man-y charms a-bout you;

a-bove all, I want my arms a-bout you.

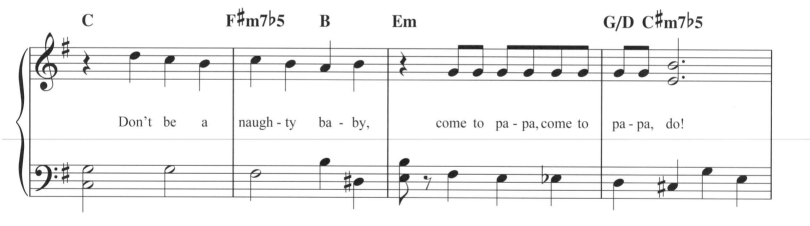

Don't be a naugh-ty ba-by, come to pa-pa, come to pa-pa, do!

My sweet em-brace - a-ble you!

EMILY

from the MGM Motion Picture THE AMERICANIZATION OF EMILY

Music by JOHNNY MANDEL
Words by JOHNNY MERCER

Moderately slow, with freedom

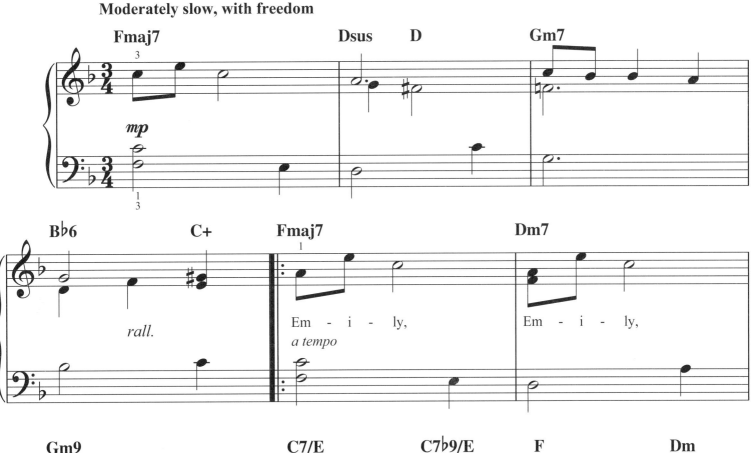

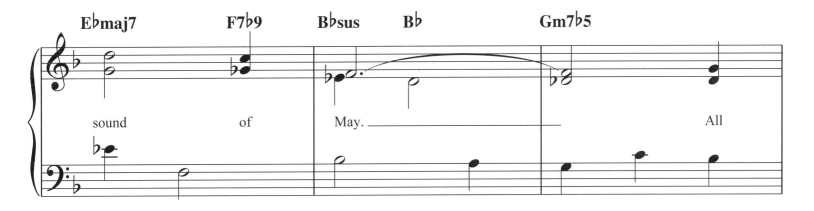

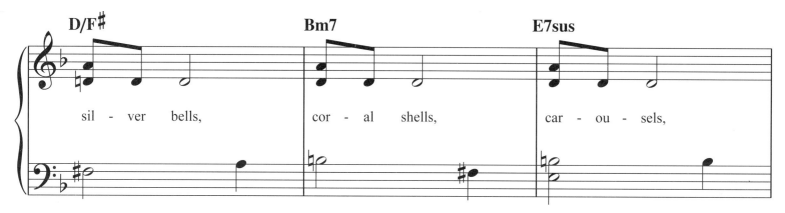

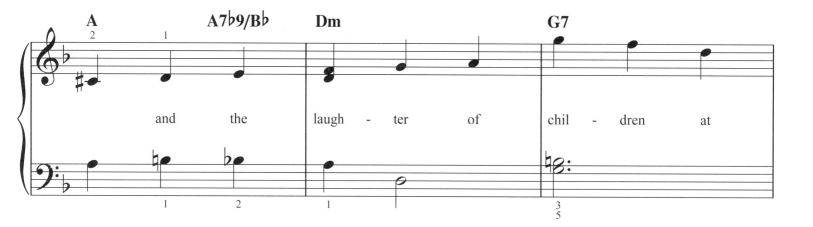

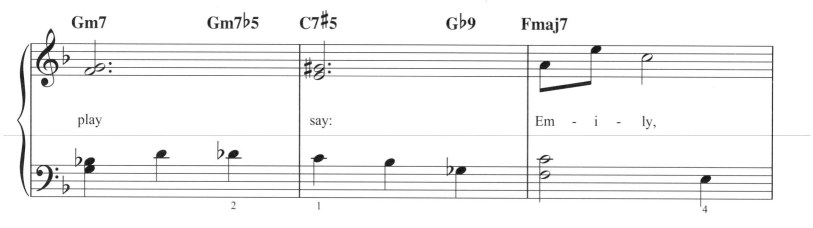

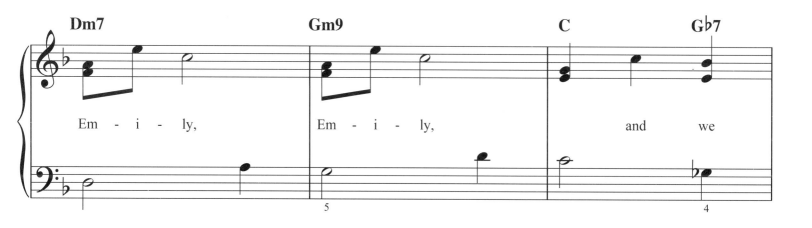

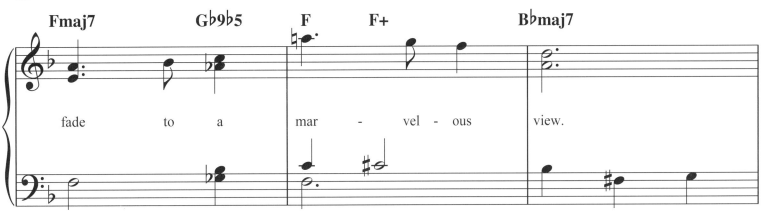

Fmaj7 **G♭9♭5** **F** **F+** **B♭maj7**

fade to a mar - vel - ous view.

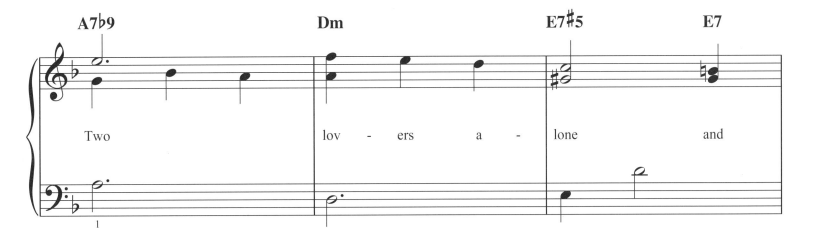

A7♭9 **Dm** **E7♯5** **E7**

Two lov - ers a - lone and

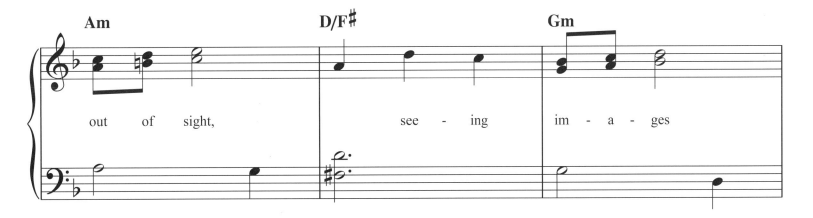

Am **D/F♯** **Gm**

out of sight, see - ing im - a - ges

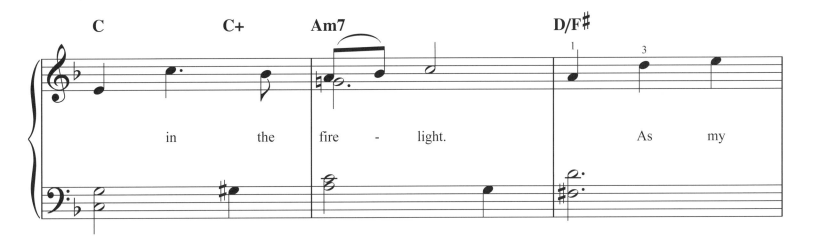

C **C+** **Am7** **D/F♯**

in the fire - light. As my

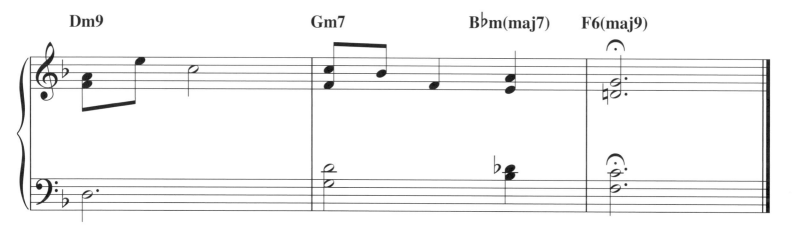

ESTATE

Music by BRUNO MARTINO
Lyrics by BRUNO BRIGHETTI

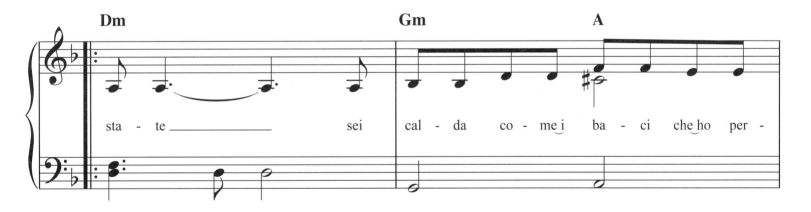

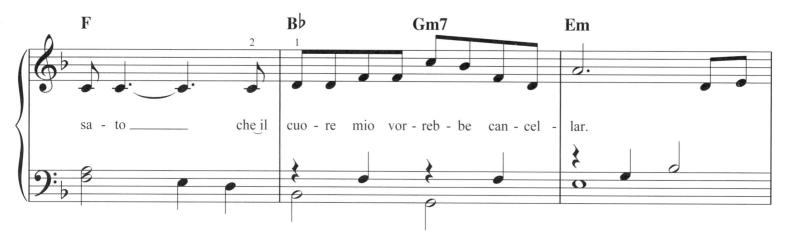

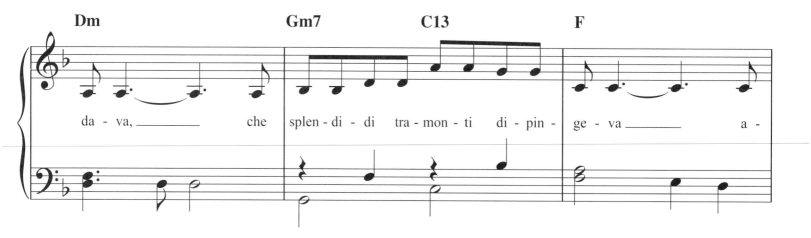

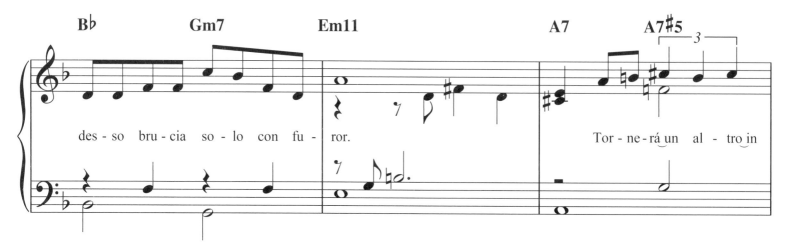

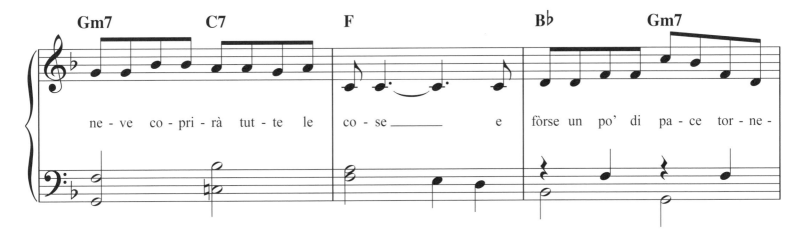

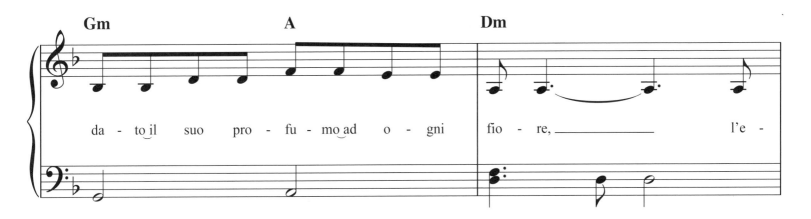

65

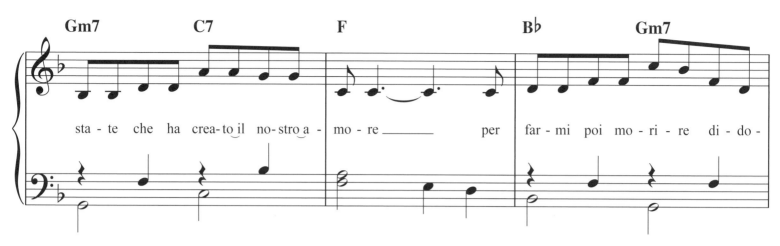

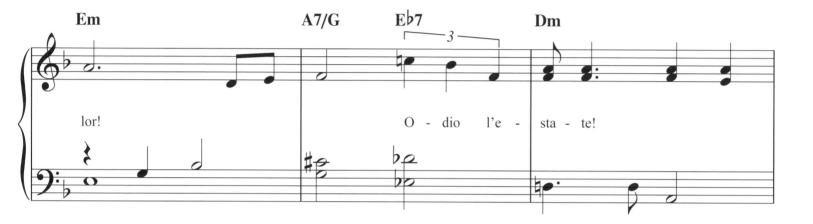

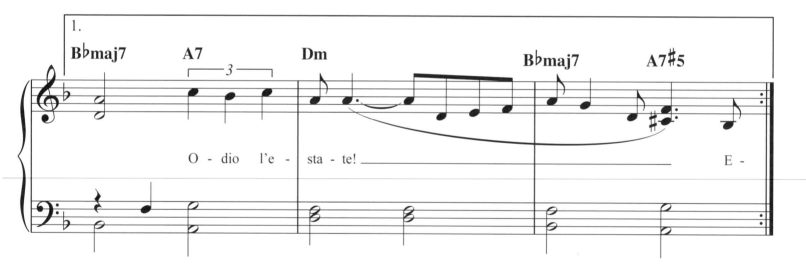

FOOTPRINTS

By WAYNE SHORTER

Moderate Swing Waltz

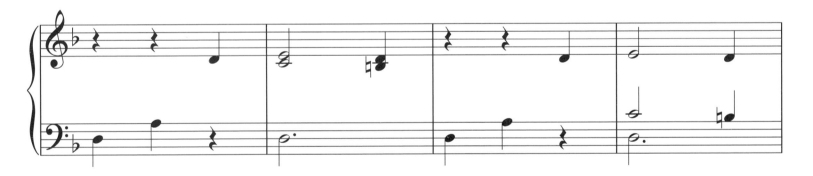

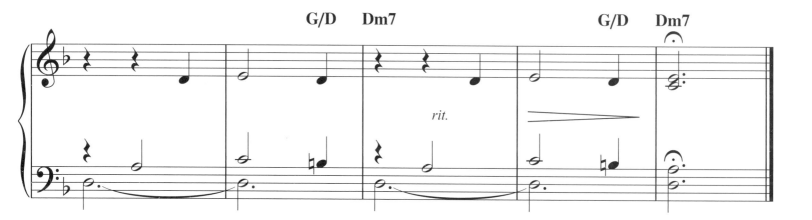

FOUR

By MILES DAVIS

Medium Swing

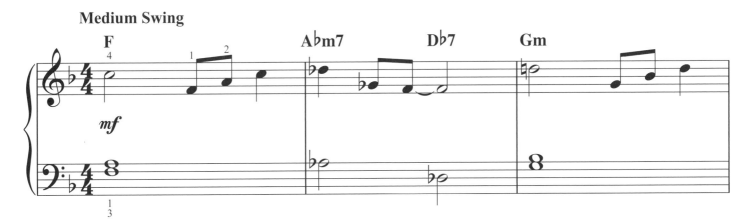

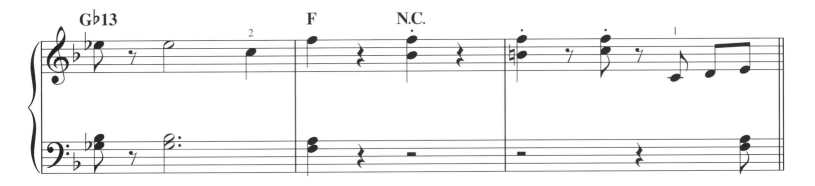

GENTLE RAIN
from the Motion Picture THE GENTLE RAIN

Music by LUIZ BONFA
Words by MATT DUBEY

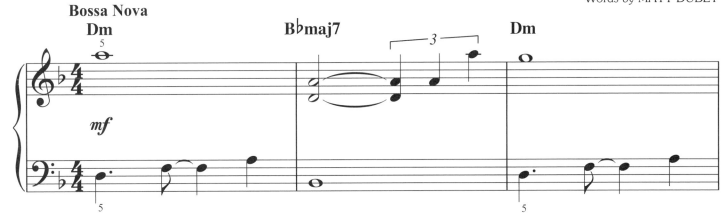

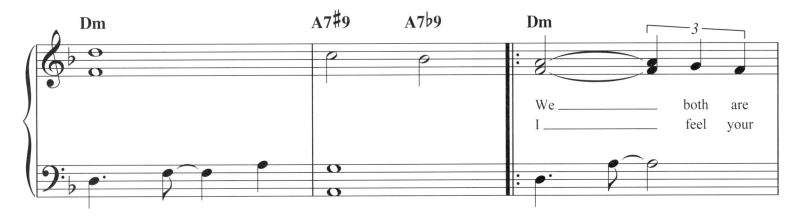

We _____ both are
I _____ feel your

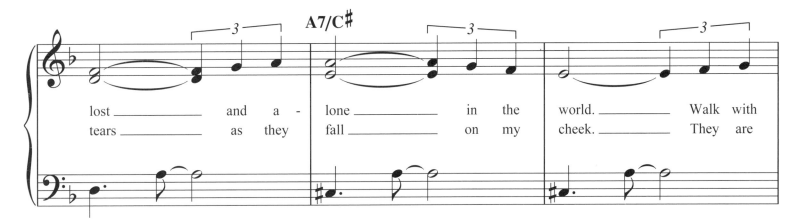

lost _____ and a-
tears _____ as they

lone _____ in the
fall _____ on my

world. _____ Walk with
cheek. _____ They are

Cm   E♭   F9   B♭6

me _____ in the gen - tle rain. _____
warm _____ like the gen - tle rain. _____

Bm7♭5   E7

Don't _____ be a - fraid; _____ I've a
Come, _____ lit - tle one, _____ you've got

Am7♭5   D7   Gm7♭5

hand _____ for your hand, _____ and I will _____ be your
me _____ in the world, _____ and our love _____ will be

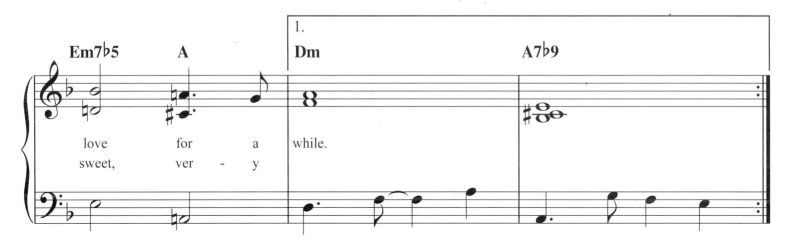

Em7♭5   A   1. Dm   A7♭9

love for a while.
sweet, ver - y

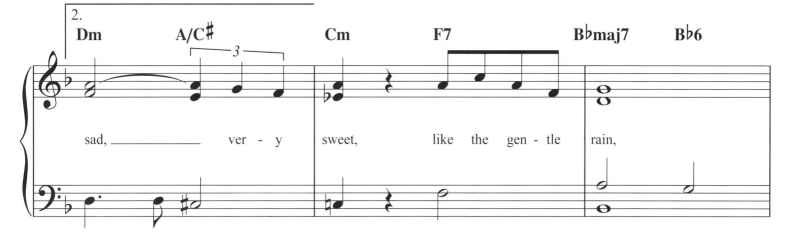

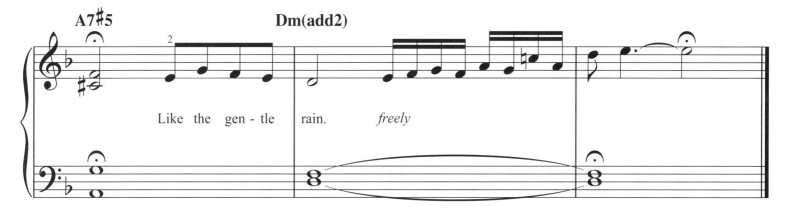

HAVE YOU MET MISS JONES?

From I'D RATHER BE RIGHT

Words by LORENZ HART
Music by RICHARD RODGERS

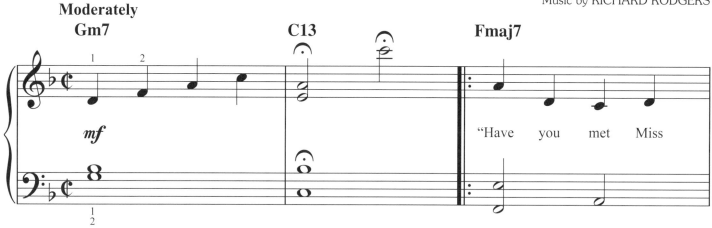

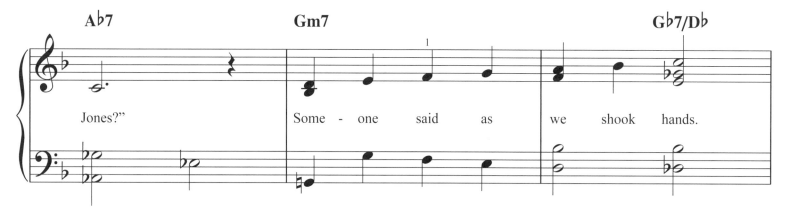

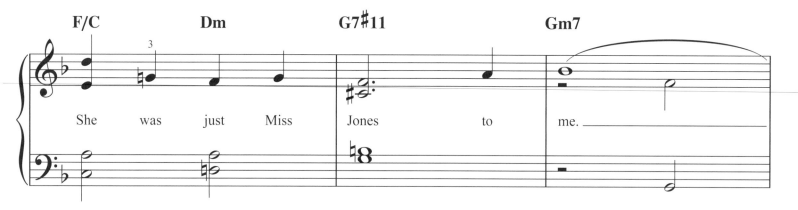

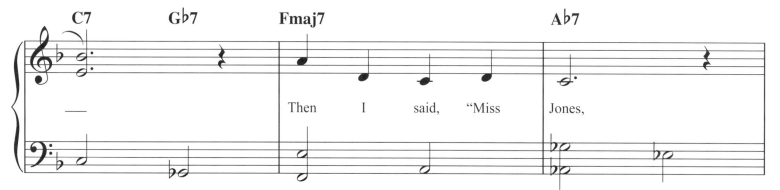

74

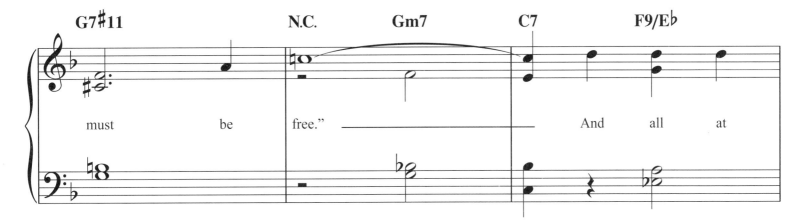

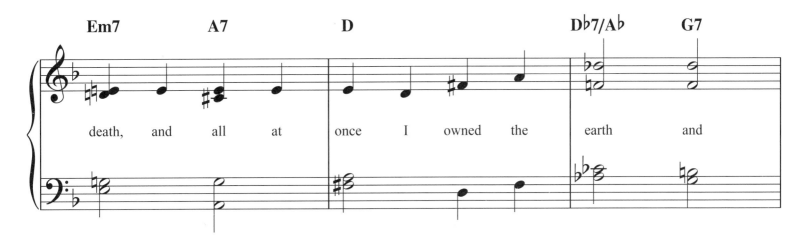

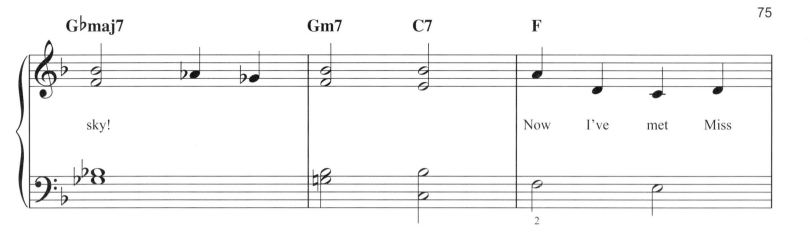

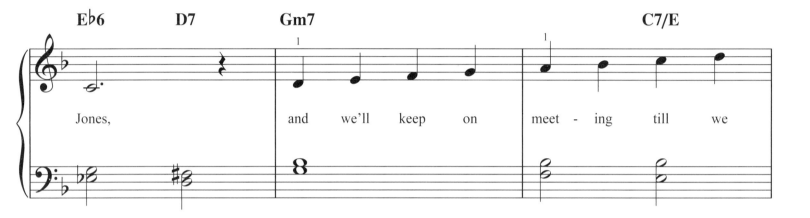

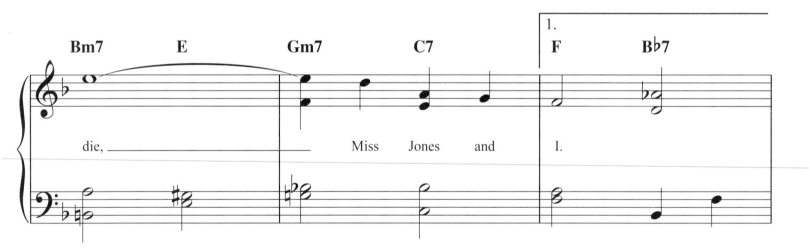

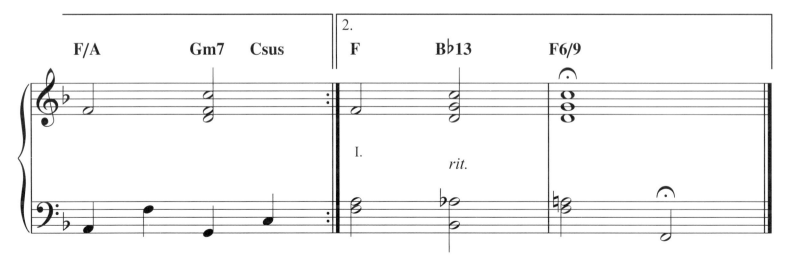

GOOD BAIT

By TADD DAMERON
and COUNT BASIE

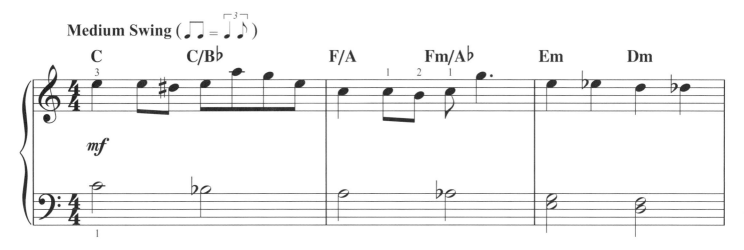

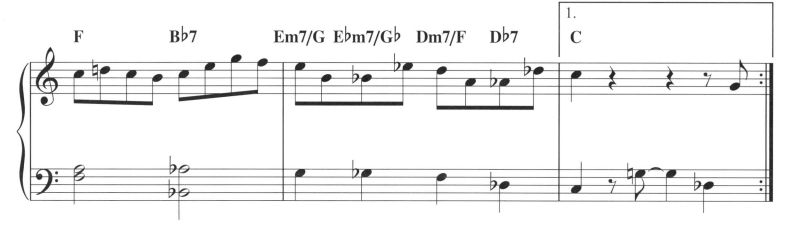

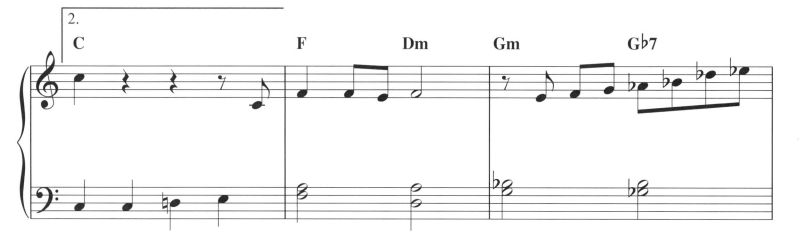

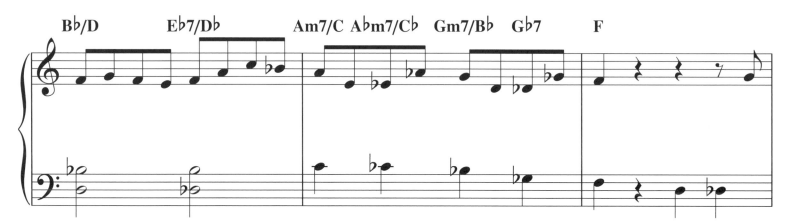

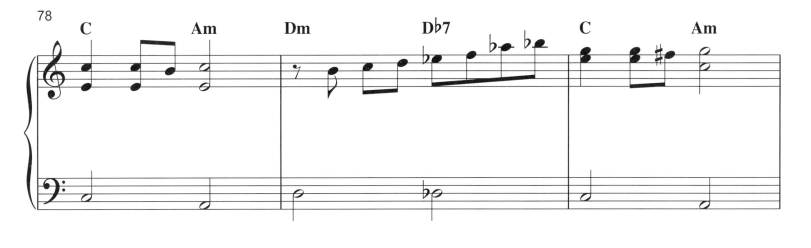

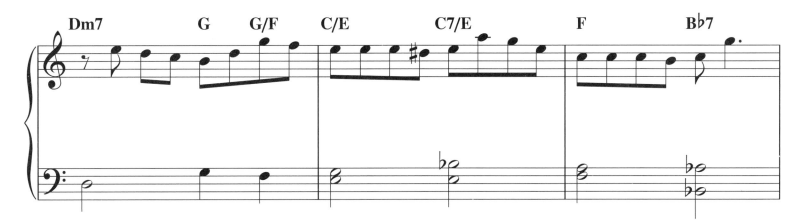

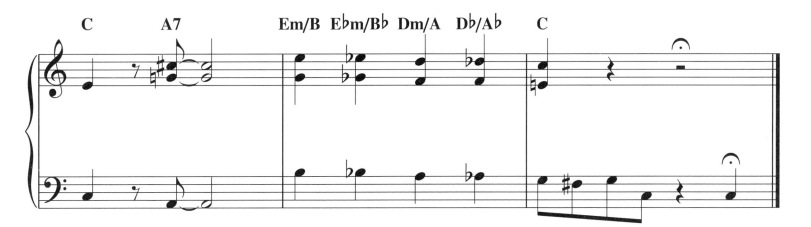

HONEYSUCKLE ROSE

from AIN'T MISBEHAVIN'

Words by ANDY RAZAF
Music by THOMAS "FATS" WALLER

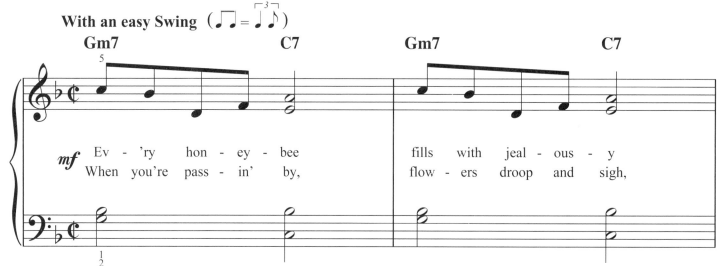

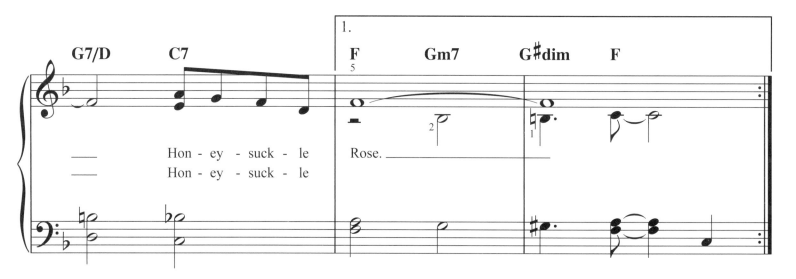

80

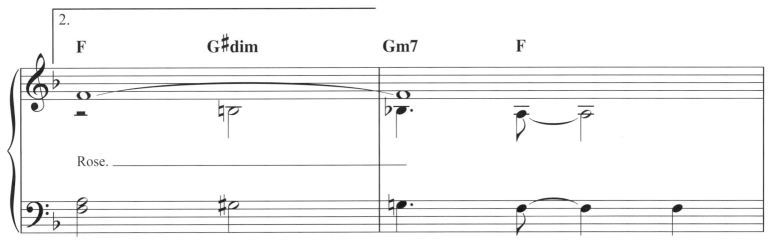

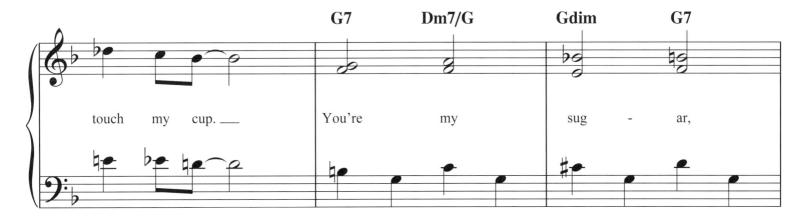

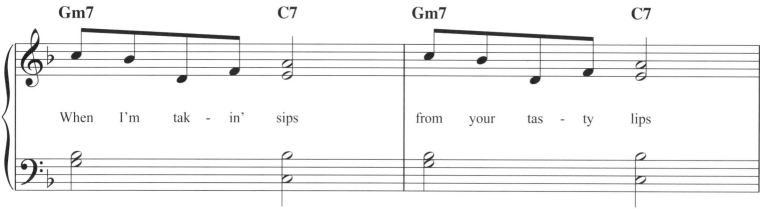

When I'm tak - in' sips   from your tas - ty lips

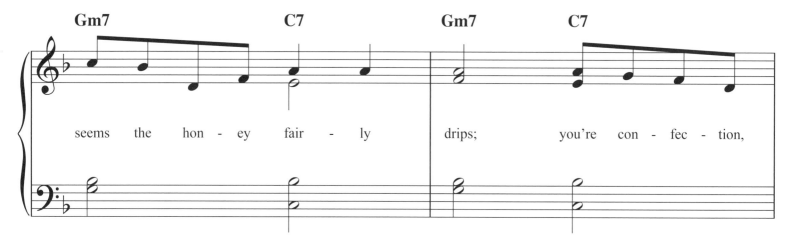

seems the hon - ey fair - ly   drips;   you're con - fec - tion,

good - ness knows, _____   Hon - ey - suck - le

Rose.

GOODBYE PORK PIE HAT

By CHARLES MINGUS

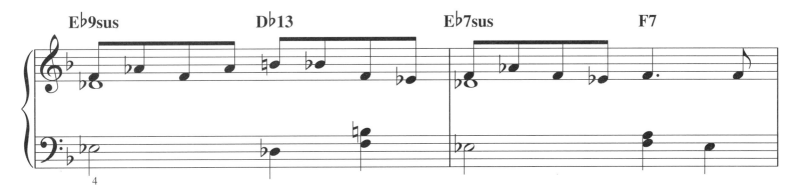

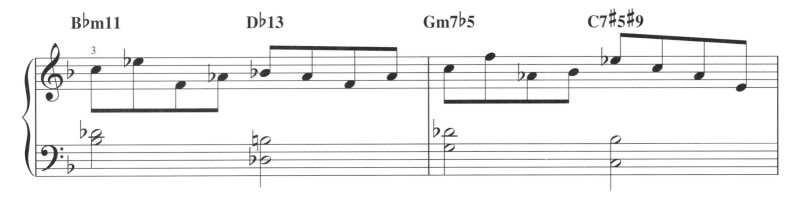

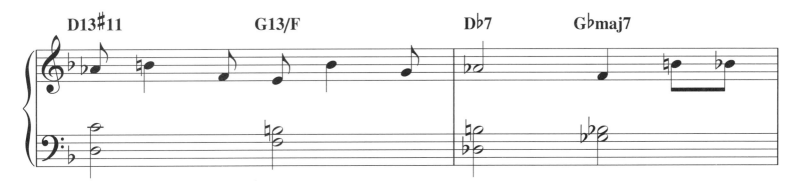

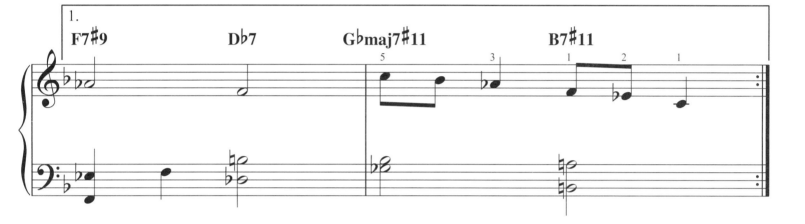

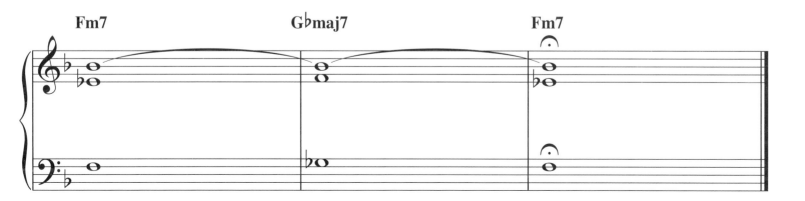

I REMEMBER YOU

from the Paramount Picture THE FLEET'S IN

Words by JOHNNY MERCER
Music by VICTOR SCHERTZINGER

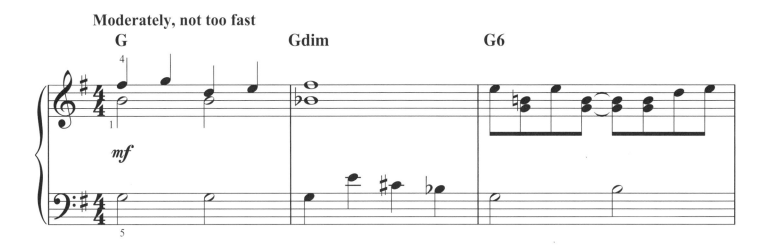

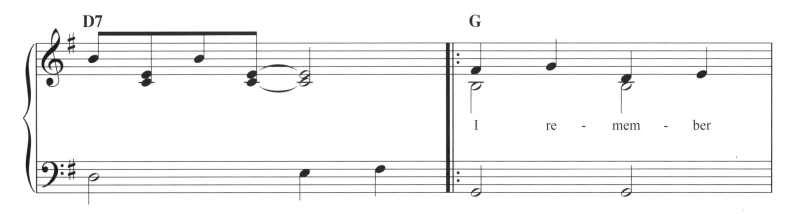

85

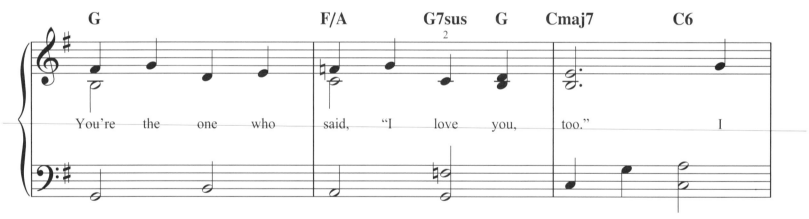

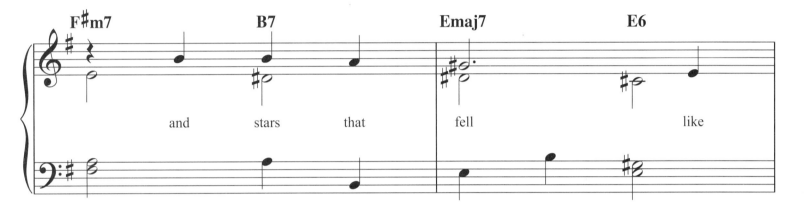

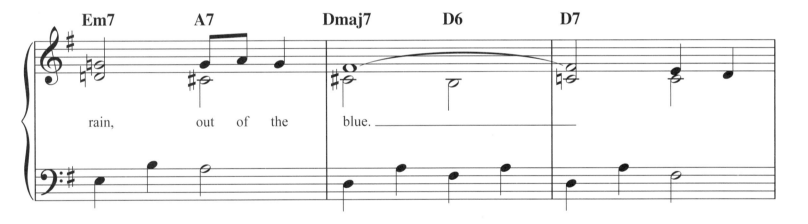

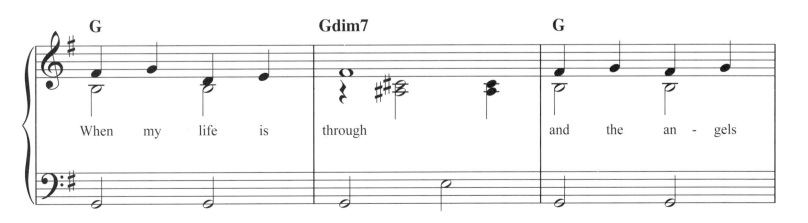

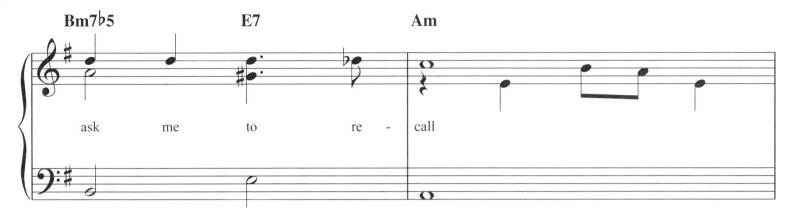

ask me to re - call

the thrill of them all, then I shall

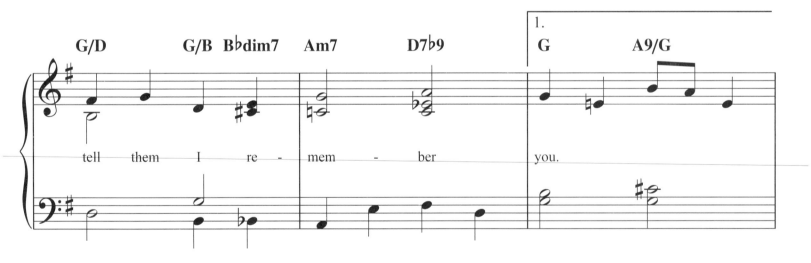

tell them I re - mem - ber you.

you.

KILLER JOE

By BENNY GOLSON

Medium Swing

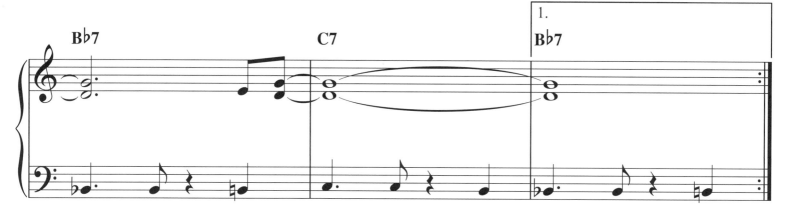

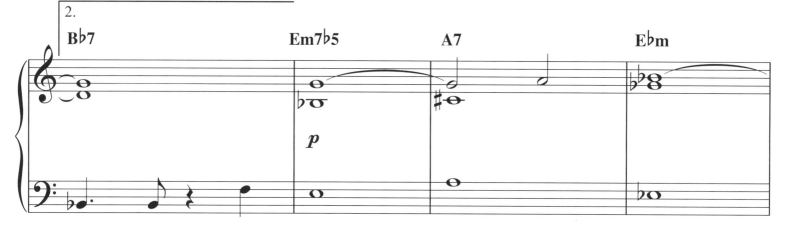

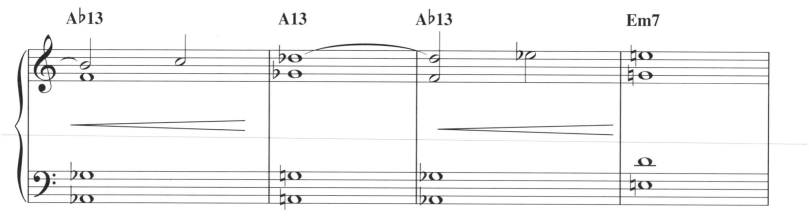

90

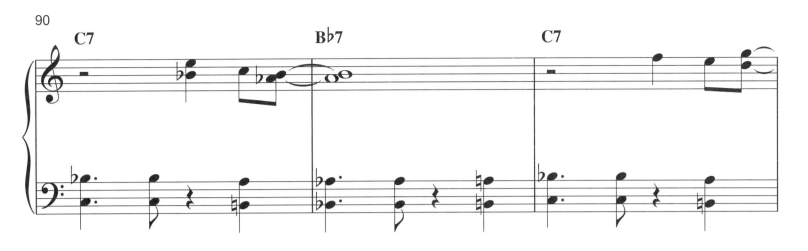

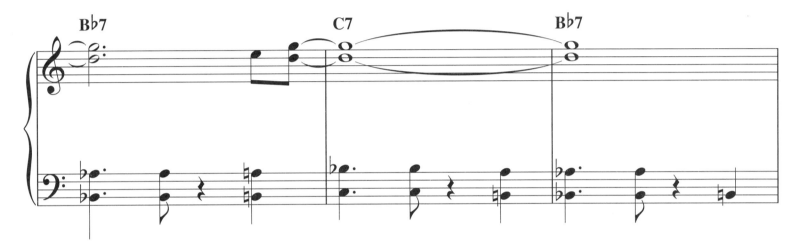

I'M GETTING SENTIMENTAL OVER YOU

Words by NED WASHINGTON
Music by GEORGE BASSMAN

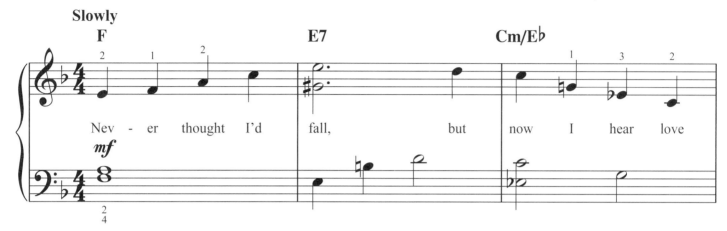

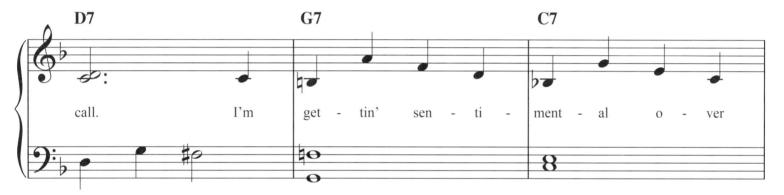

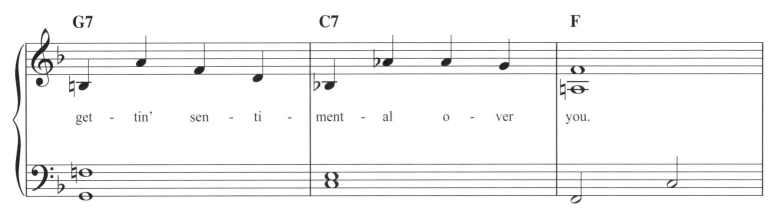

get - tin' sen - ti - ment - al o - ver you.

I thought I was hap - py, I could

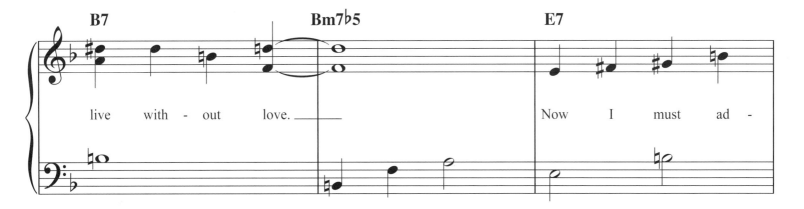

live with - out love. Now I must ad -

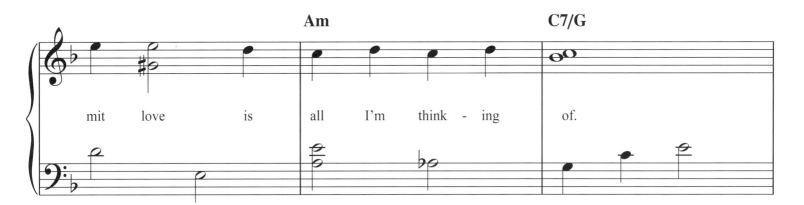

mit love is all I'm think - ing of.

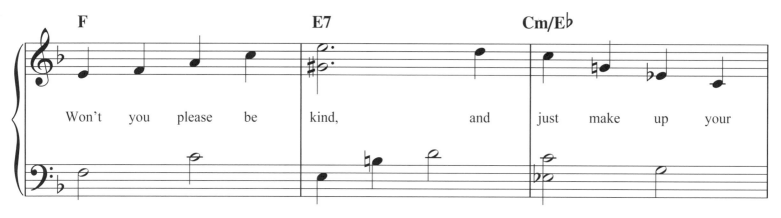

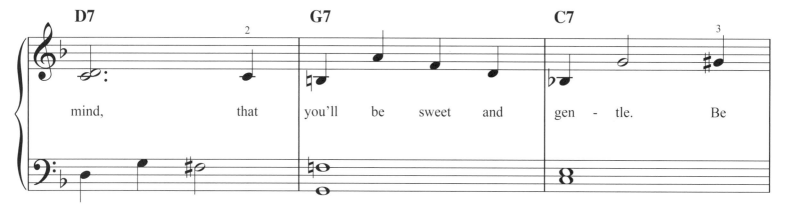

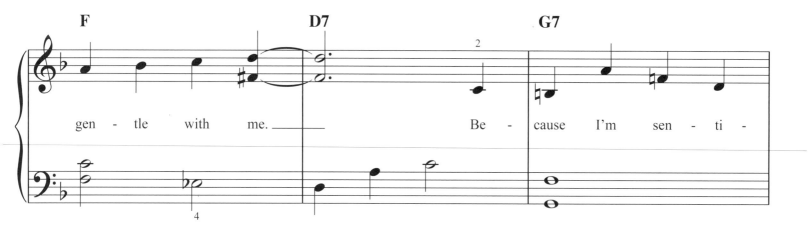

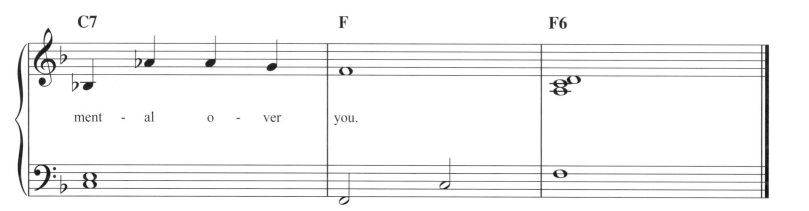

IN WALKED BUD

By Thelonious Monk

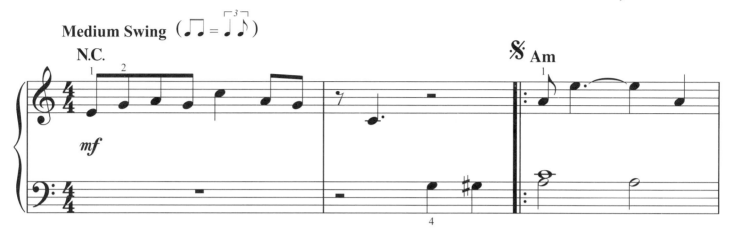

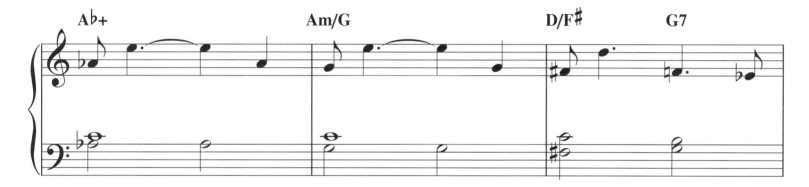

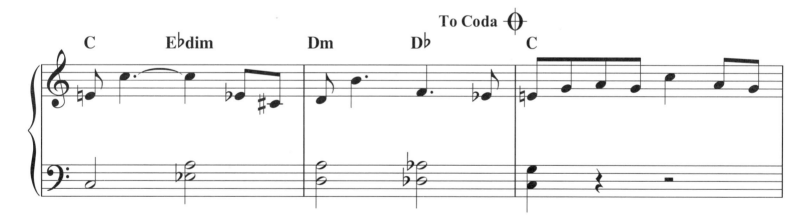

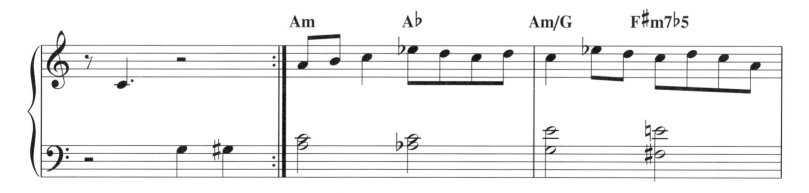

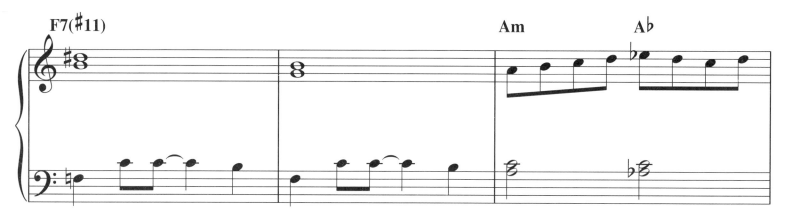

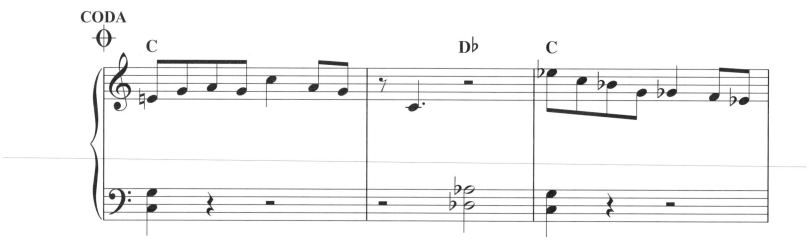

IN YOUR OWN SWEET WAY

By DAVE BRUBECK

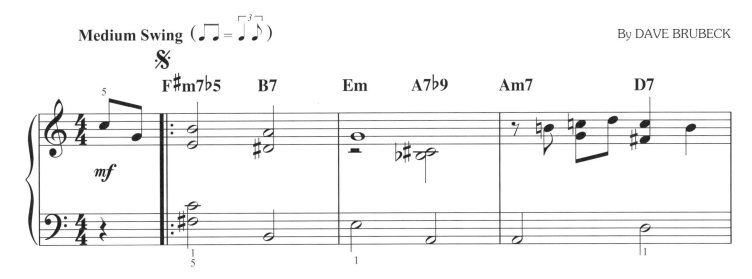

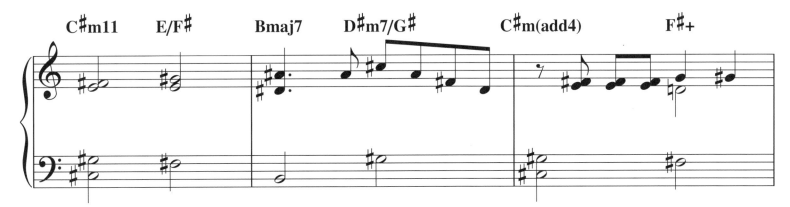

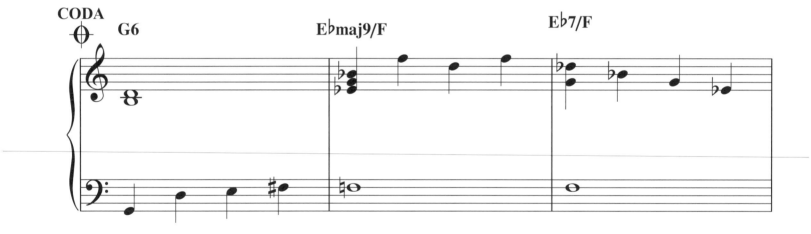

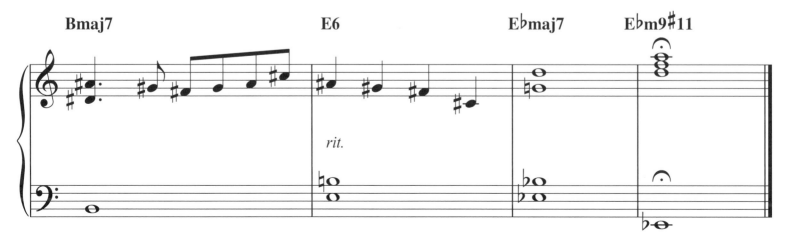

LITTLE SUNFLOWER

By FREDDIE HUBBARD

Medium Latin

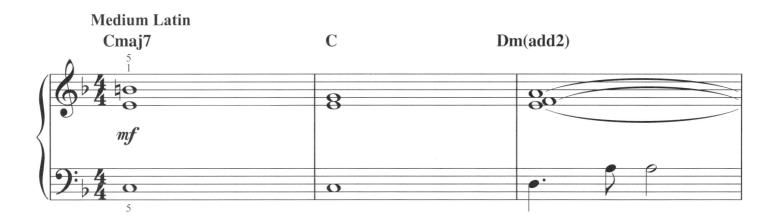

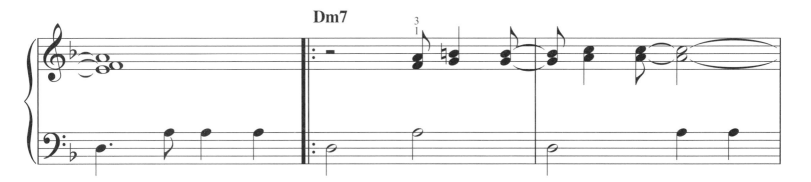

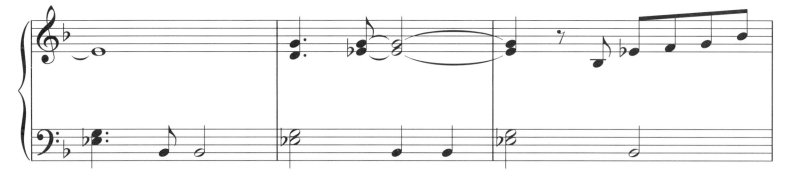

Dm7

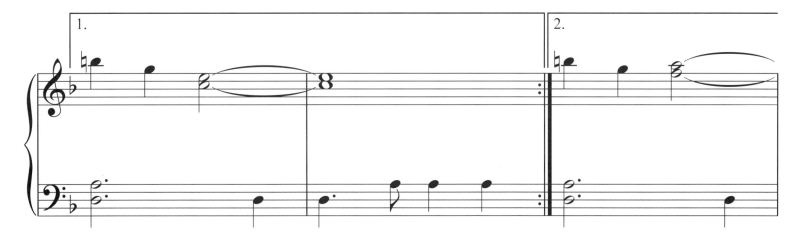

Cmaj7

Dm(add2)

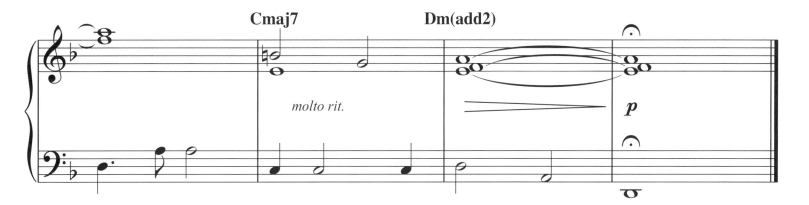

molto rit.

p

LULLABY OF BIRDLAND

Words by GEORGE DAVID WEISS
Music by GEORGE SHEARING

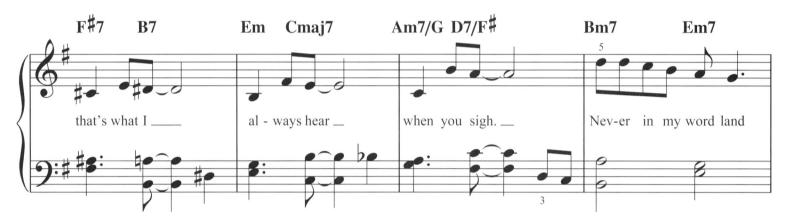

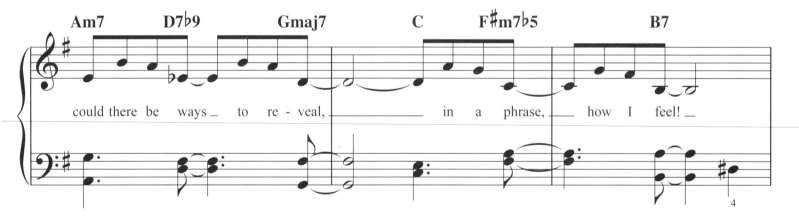

when they love? _ That's the kind of mag - ic mu - sic we make _ with our lips _

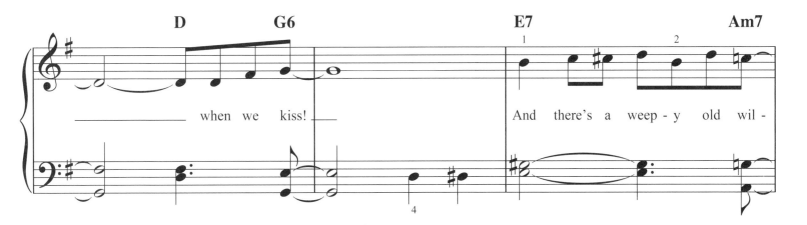

_____ when we kiss! __ And there's a weep - y old wil -

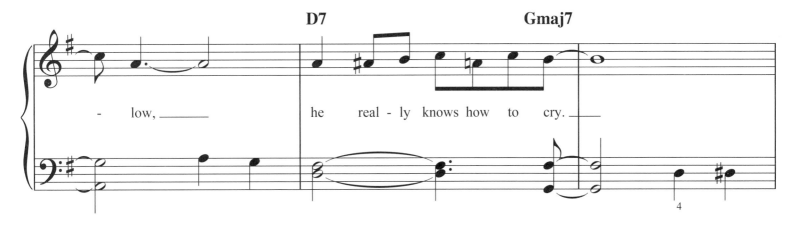

- low, _____ he real - ly knows how to cry. __

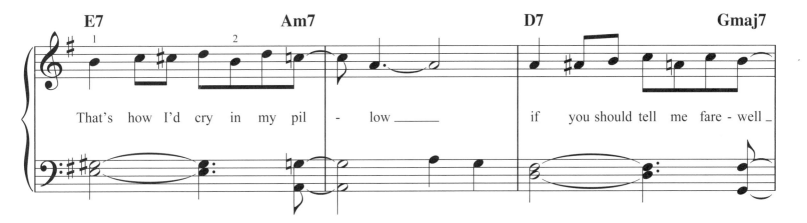

That's how I'd cry in my pil - low _____ if you should tell me fare - well _

remaining

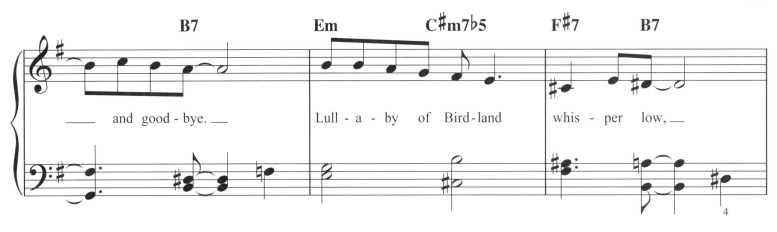

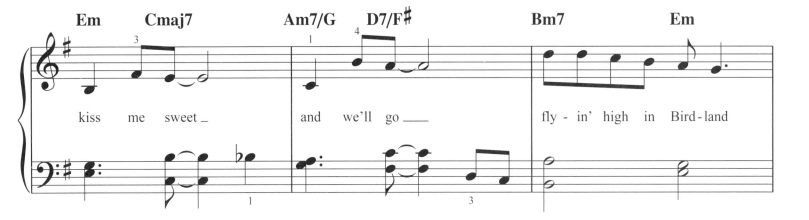

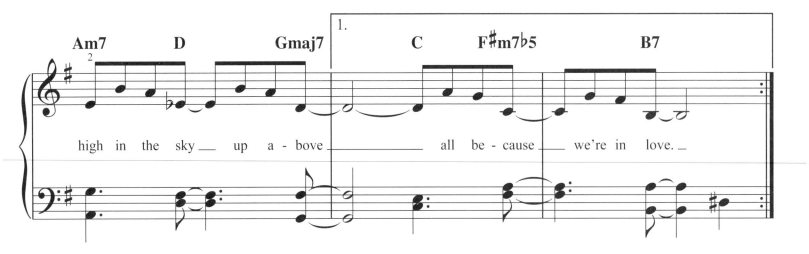

MERCY, MERCY, MERCY

By JOSEF ZAWINUL

Slow Funky Rock

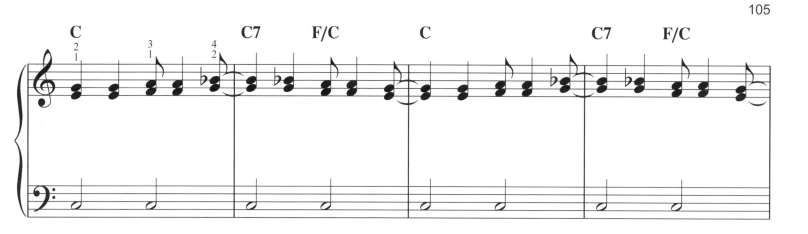

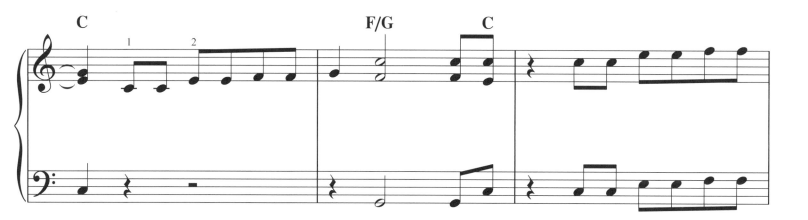

MY FOOLISH HEART
from MY FOOLISH HEART

Words by NED WASHINGTON
Music by VICTOR YOUNG

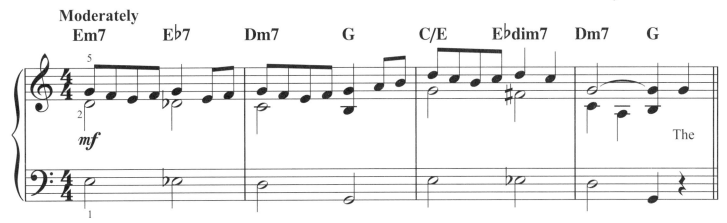

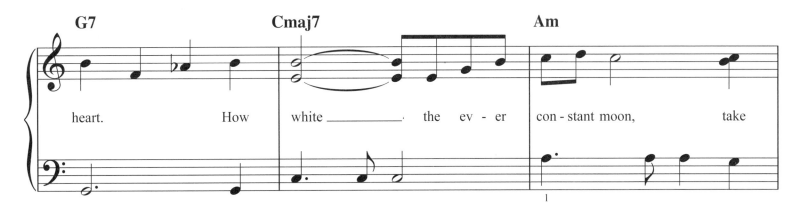

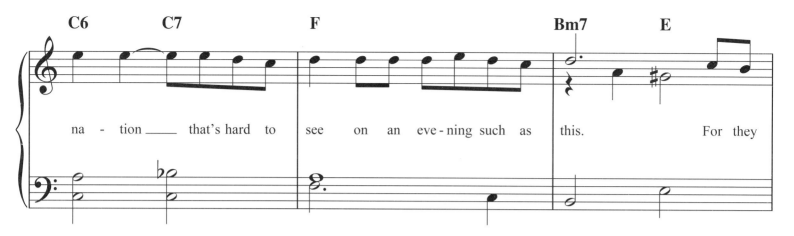

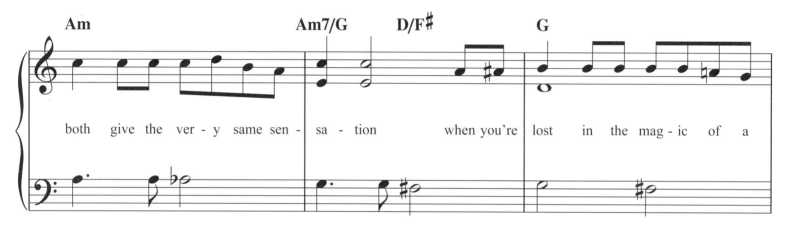

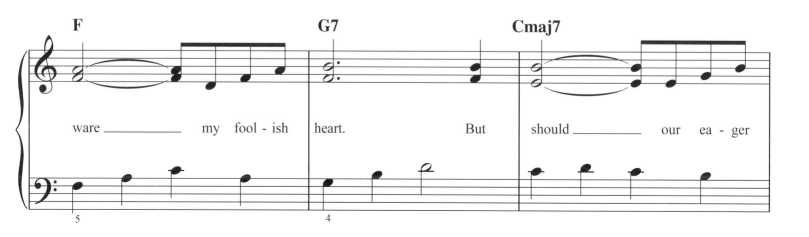

lips com-bine   then   let _____ the fire ___ start.   For

this time it is-n't fas-ci - na - tion   or a   dream that will fade and fall a -

part.   It's   love this time, it's   love, my   fool - ish

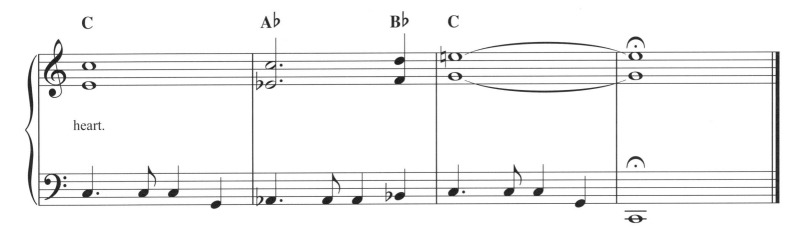

heart.

NUAGES

By DJANGO REINHARDT
and JACQUES LARUE

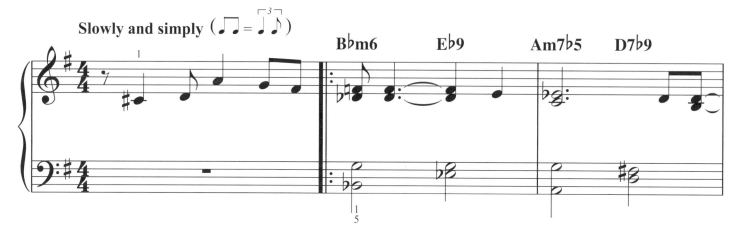

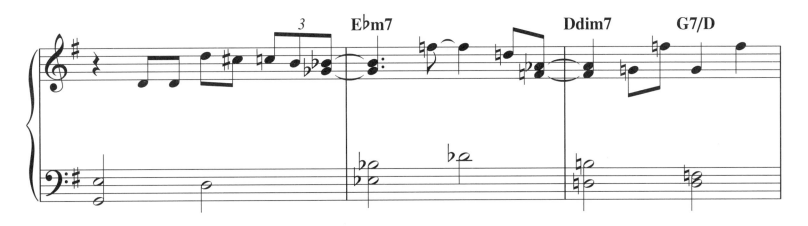

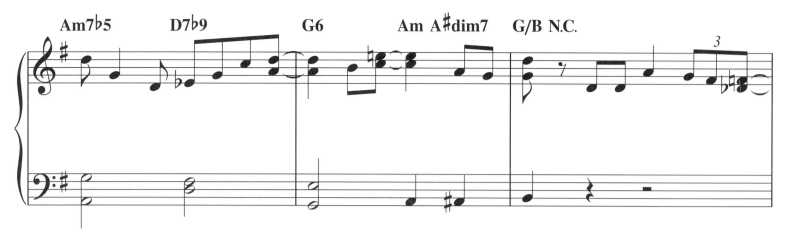

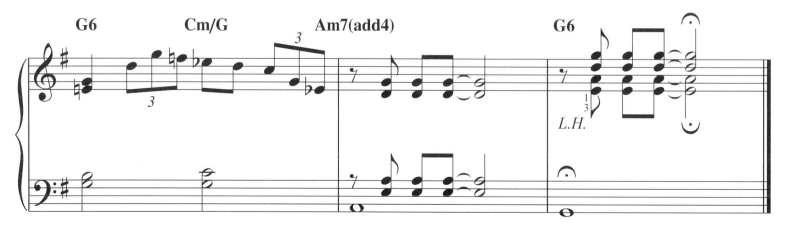

NAIMA
(Niema)

By JOHN COLTRANE

Slow Ballad

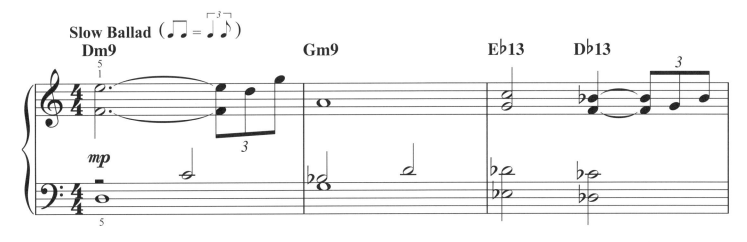

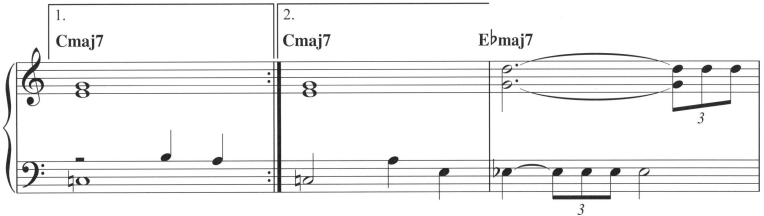

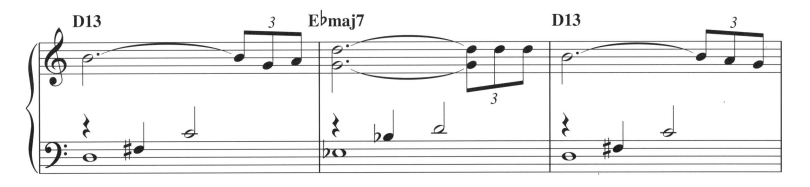

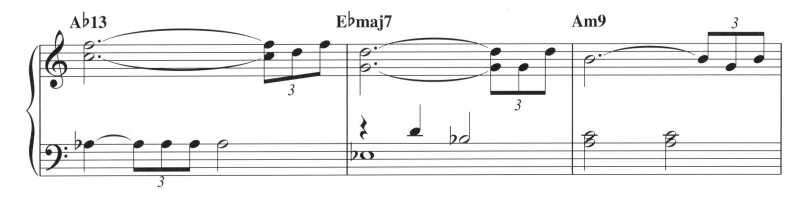

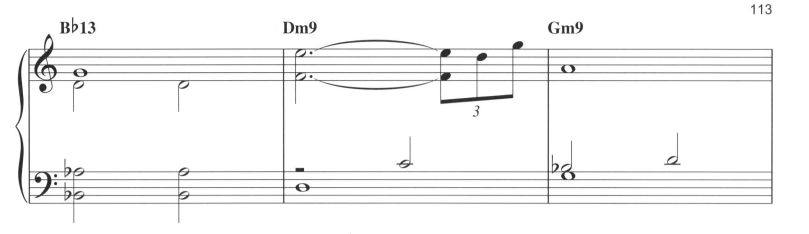

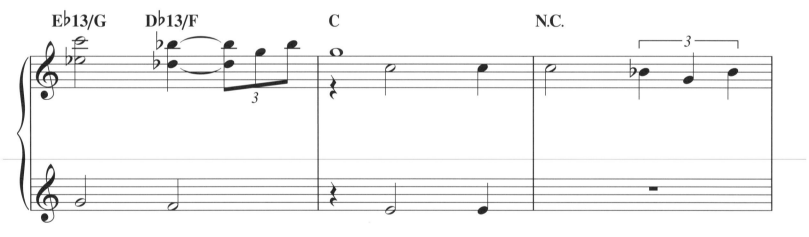

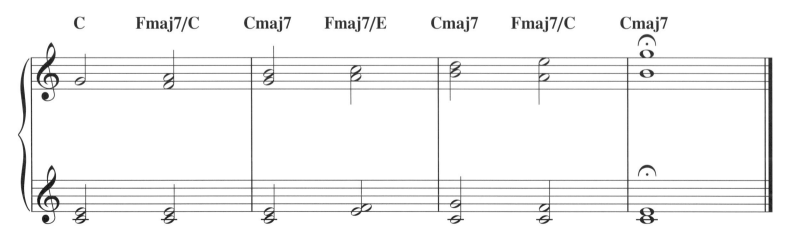

NIGHT TRAIN

Words by OSCAR WASHINGTON
and LEWIS C. SIMPKINS
Music by JIMMY FORREST

Medium Swing

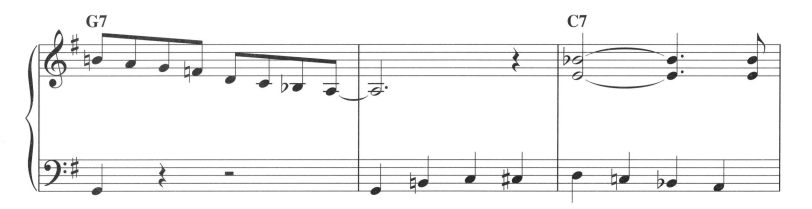

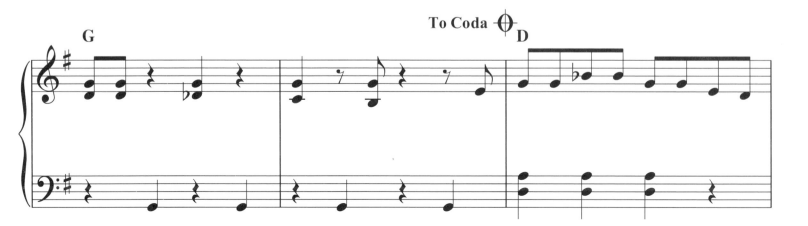

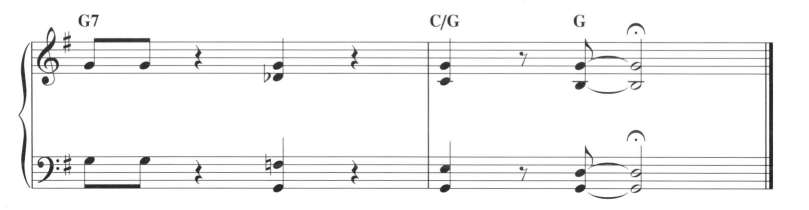

ON GREEN DOLPHIN STREET

Lyrics by NED WASHINGTON
Music by BRONISLAU KAPER

Moderately, with freedom

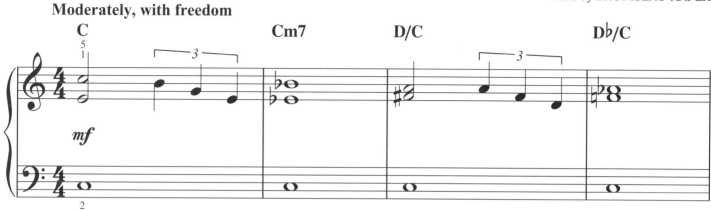

It seems like a dream, *rit.* *a tempo*

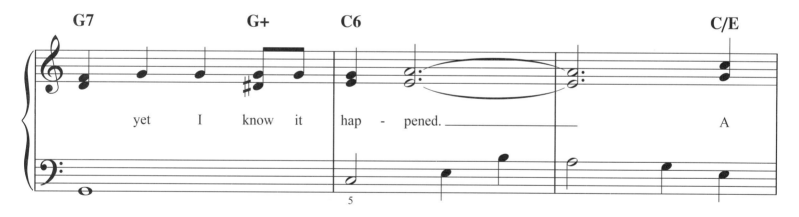

yet I know it hap - pened. _____ A

man, a maid, a kiss, and then good - bye.

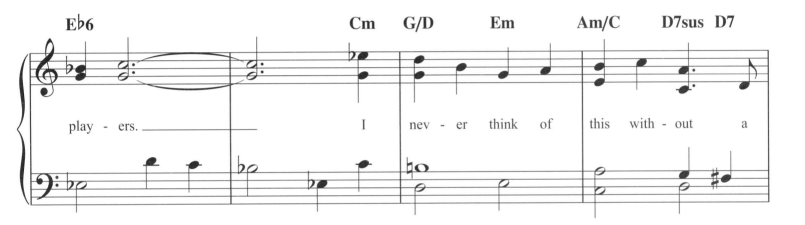

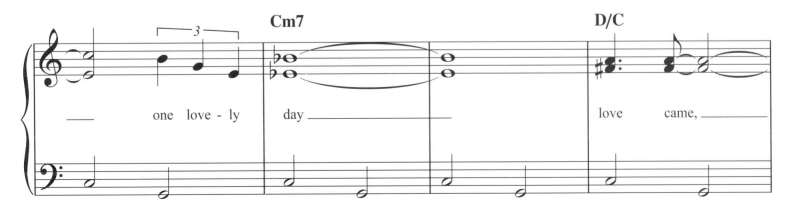

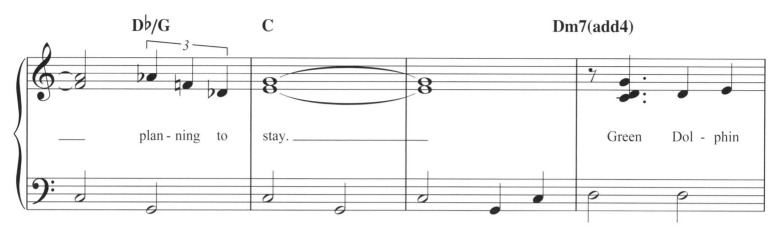

D♭/G   C   Dm7(add4)

___ plan - ning to   stay. ___   Green   Dol - phin

G7   G7♯5♭9/B   C   Fm7

Street sup - plied the   set - ting, ___   the   set - ting for

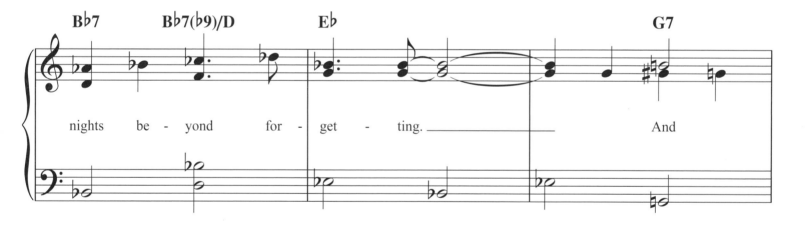

B♭7   B♭7(♭9)/D   E♭   G7

nights be - yond for - get - ting. ___   And

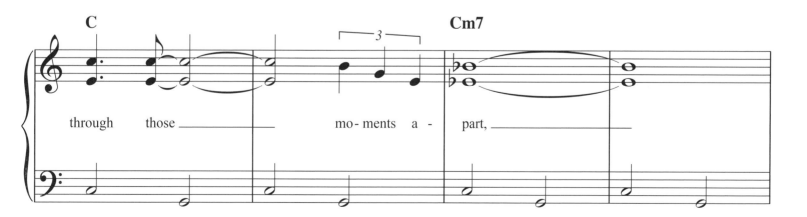

C   Cm7

through those ___   mo - ments a -   part, ___

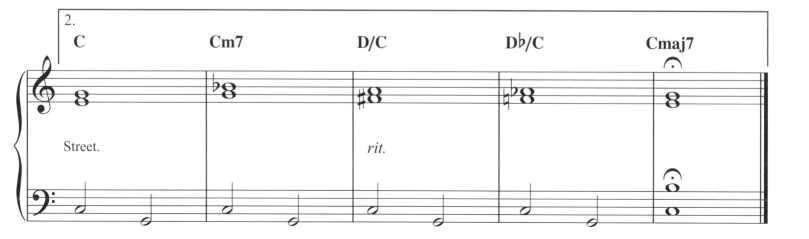

RECORDA ME

By JOE HENDERSON

123

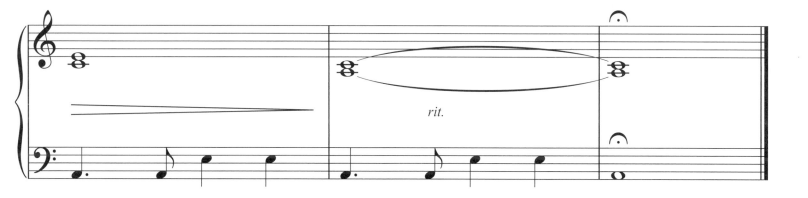

TAKE THE "A" TRAIN

Words and Music by
BILLY STRAYHORN

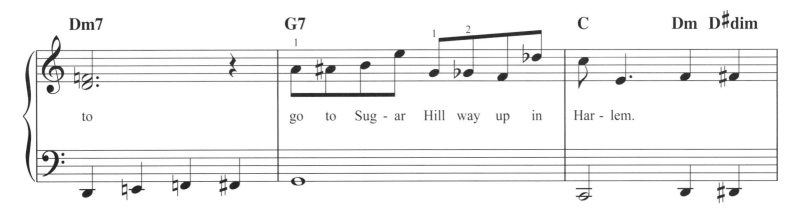

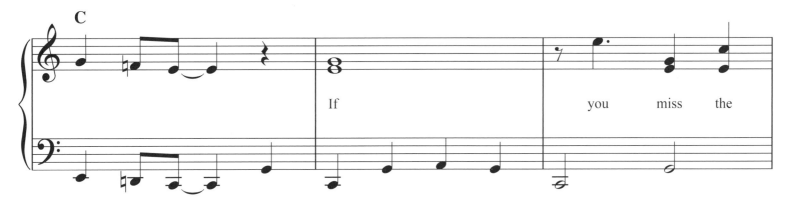

"A" train, _____ you'll

find you've missed the quick-est way to Har - lem.

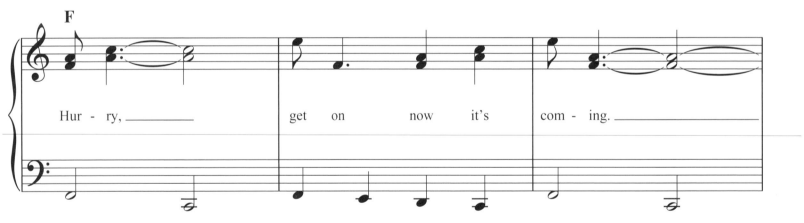

Hur - ry, _____ get on now it's com - ing. _____

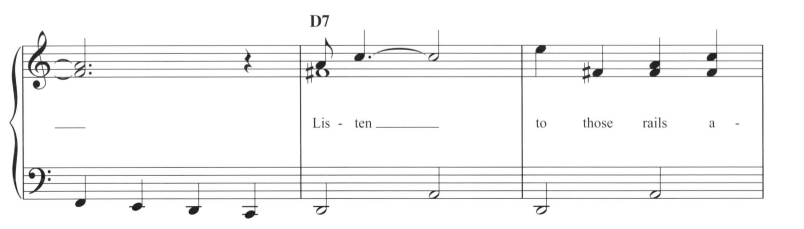

Lis - ten _____ to those rails a -

126

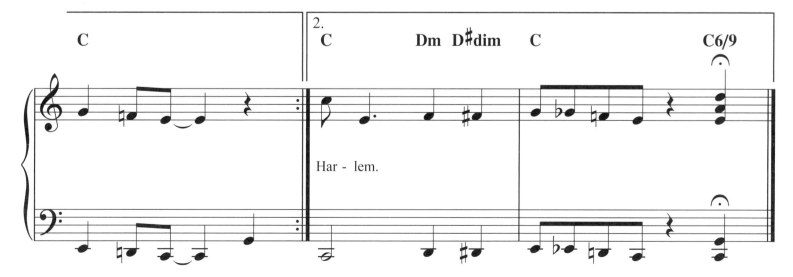

ST. THOMAS

By SONNY ROLLINS

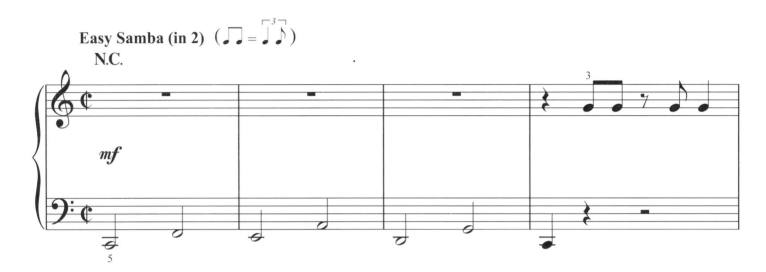

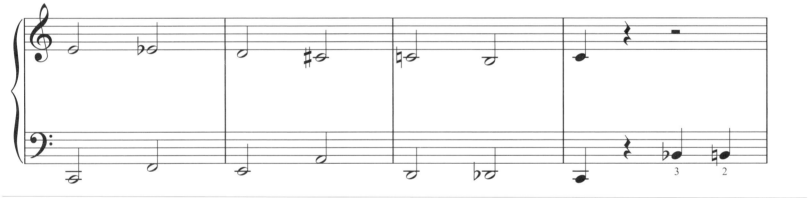

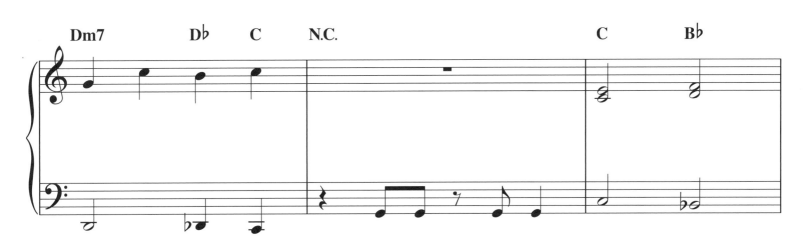

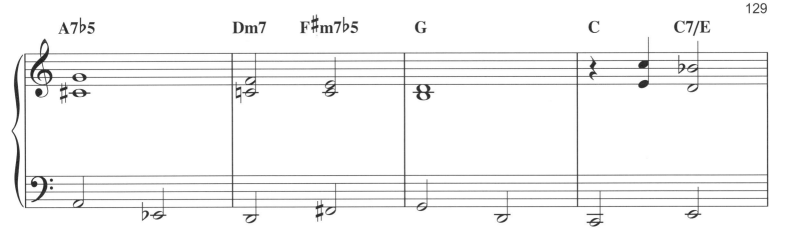

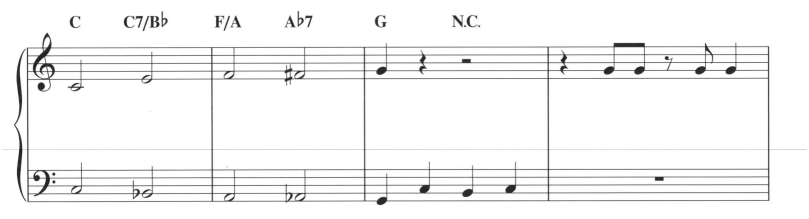

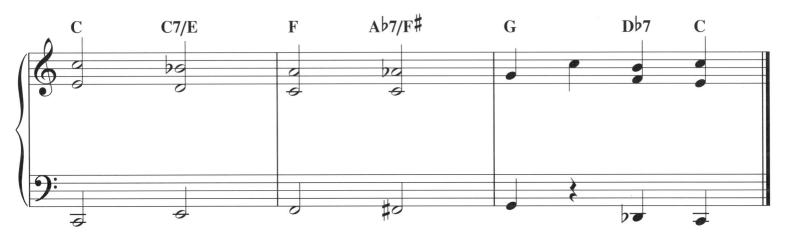

THE SHADOW OF YOUR SMILE
Love Theme from THE SANDPIPER

Music by JOHNNY MANDEL
Words by PAUL FRANCIS WEBSTER

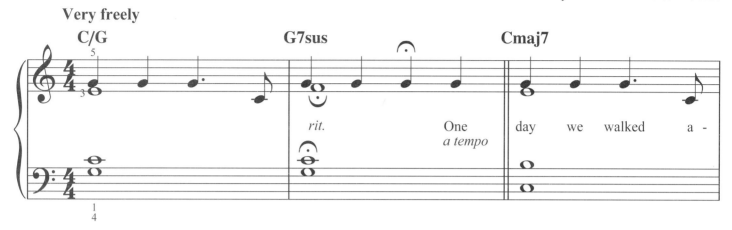

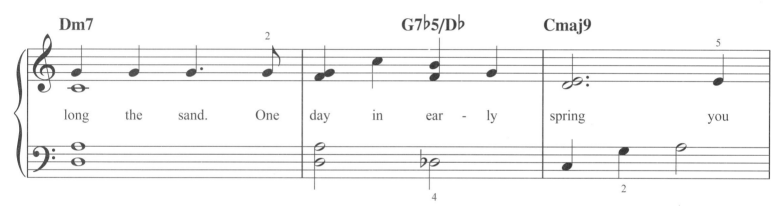

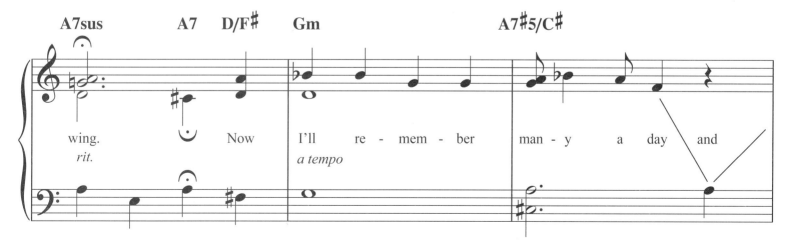

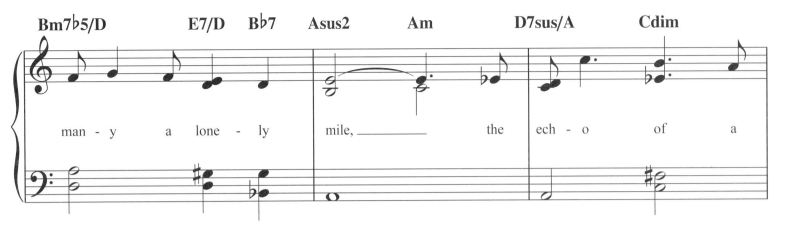

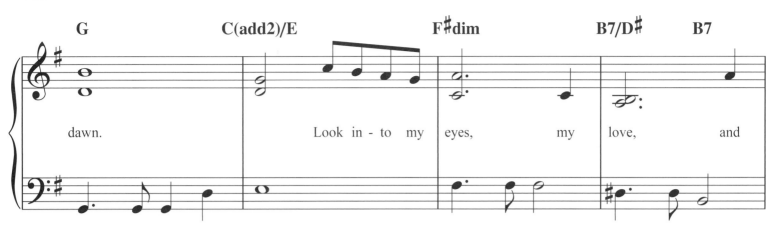

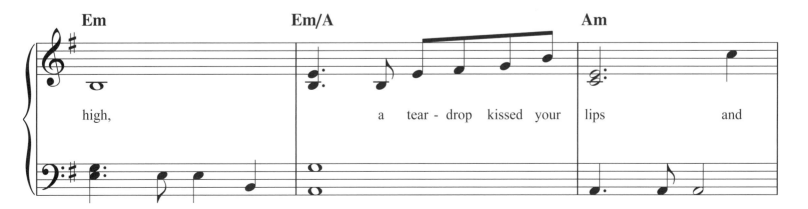

133

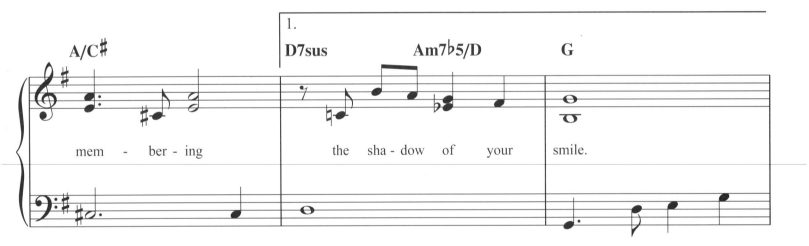

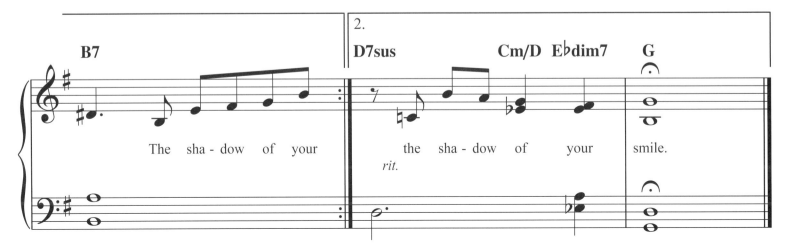

SIDEWINDER

By LEE MORGAN

G7   C7

Bm7♭5   E7   Am   Bm/E   Am   Bm/E   Am

D7   G7

G7#9   N.C.   1.   2.   G7#9

STOMPIN' AT THE SAVOY

Words by ANDY RAZAF
Music by BENNY GOODMAN,
EDGAR SAMPSON and CHICK WEBB

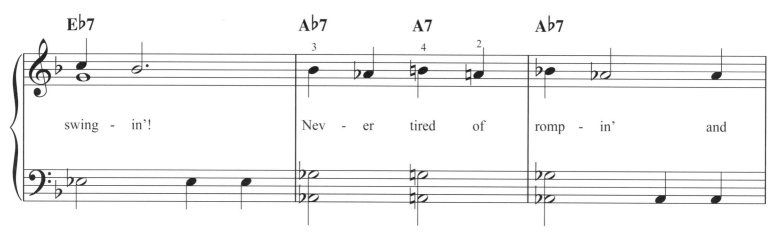

swing - in'! Nev - er tired of romp - in' and

stomp - in' with you at the Sa - voy. What joy! A per - fect hol - i -

day! Sa - voy, where we can glide and sway; Sa -

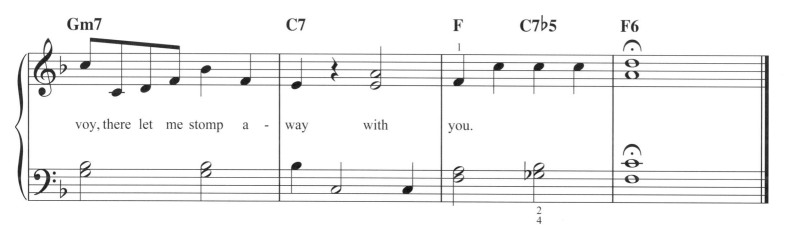

voy, there let me stomp a - way with you.

TAKE FIVE

By PAUL DESMOND

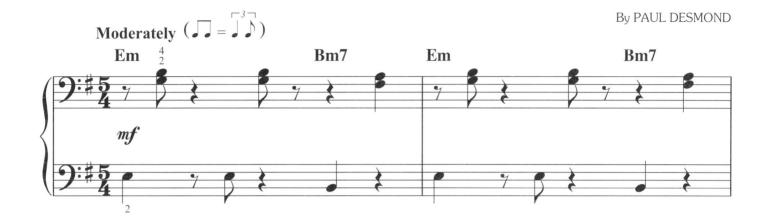

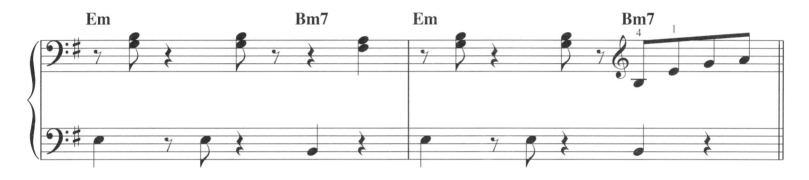

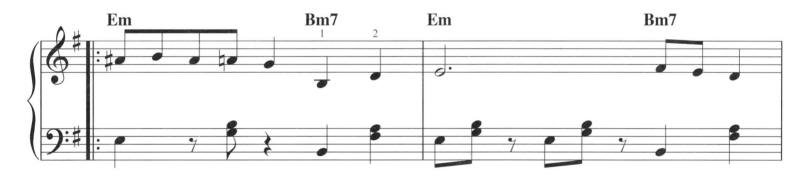

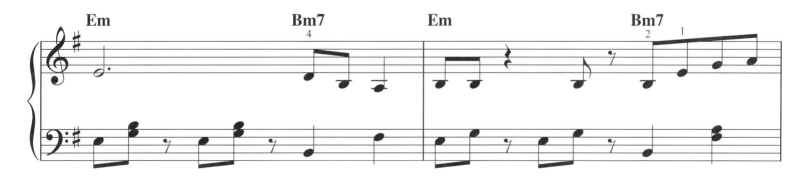

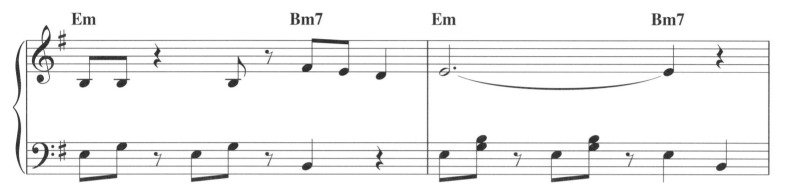

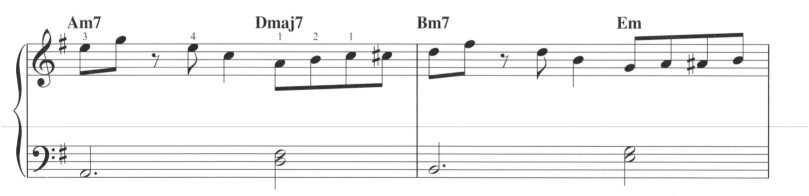

140

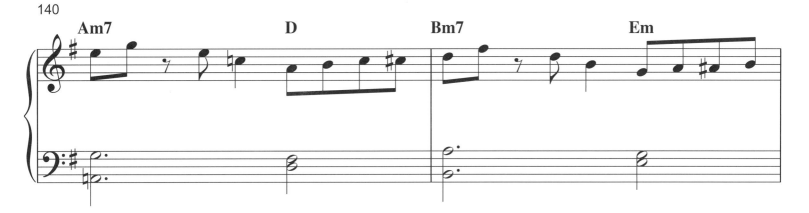

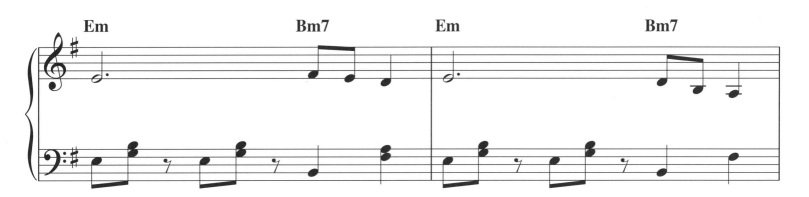

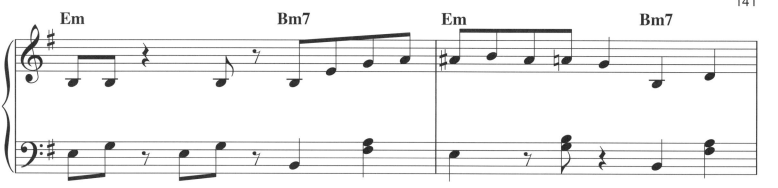

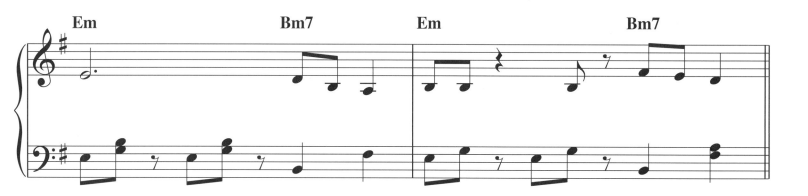

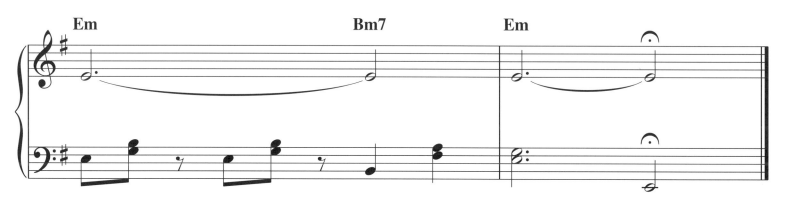

WATCH WHAT HAPPENS
from THE UMBRELLAS OF CHERBOURG

Music by MICHEL LEGRAND
Original French Text by JACQUES DEMY
English Lyrics by NORMAN GIMBEL

Slow Beguine tempo

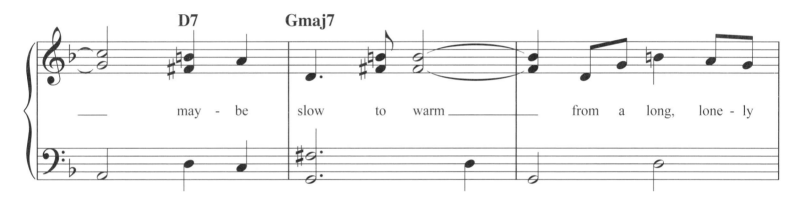

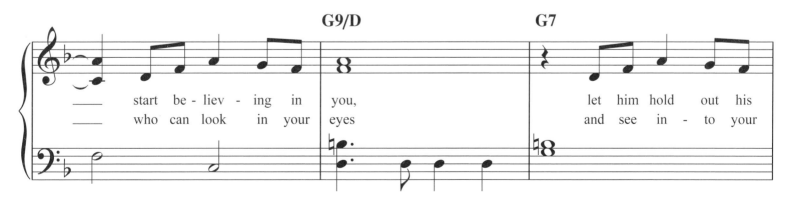

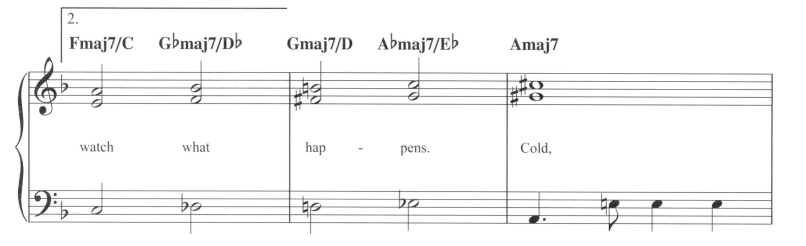

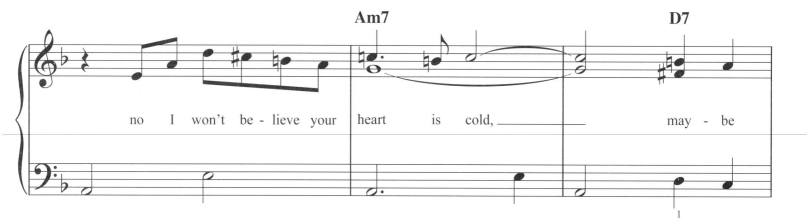

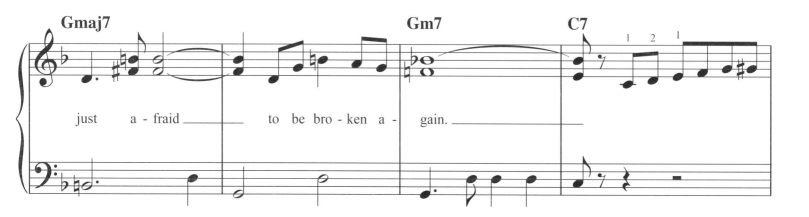

144

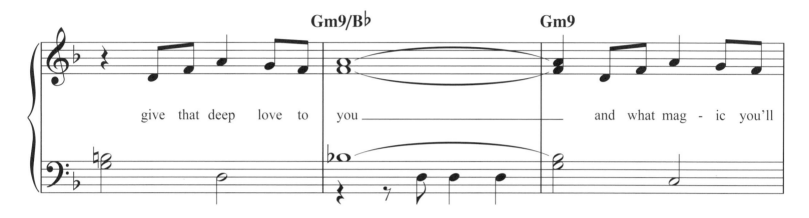

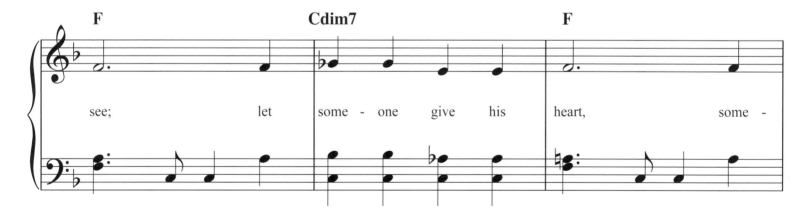

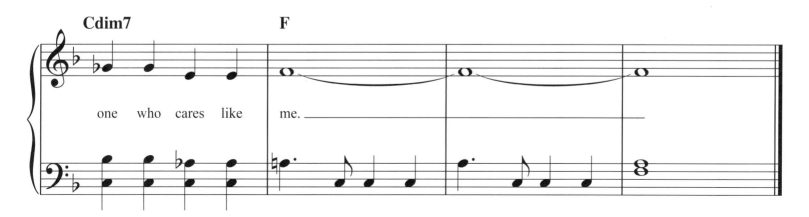

THE VERY THOUGHT OF YOU

Words and Music by
RAY NOBLE

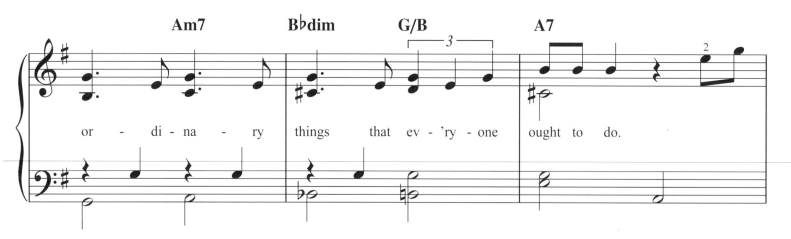

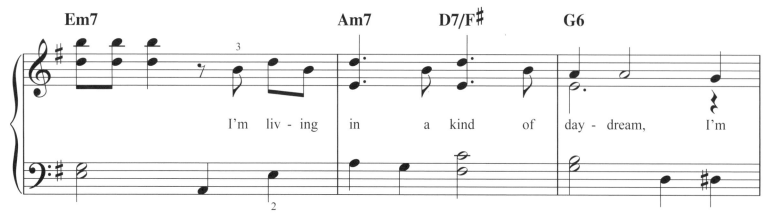

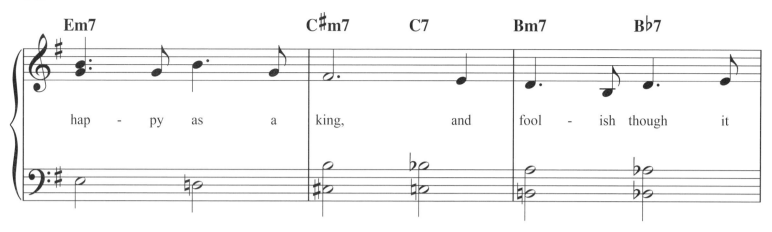

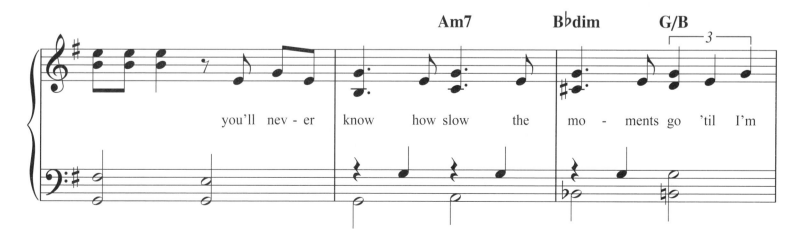

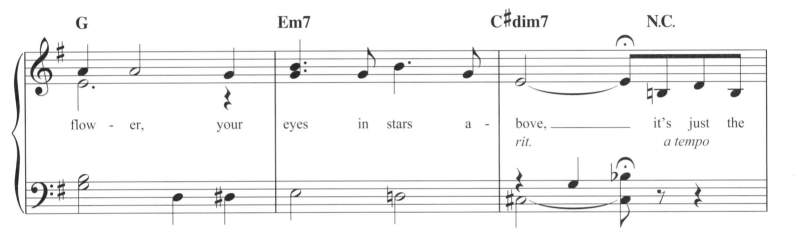

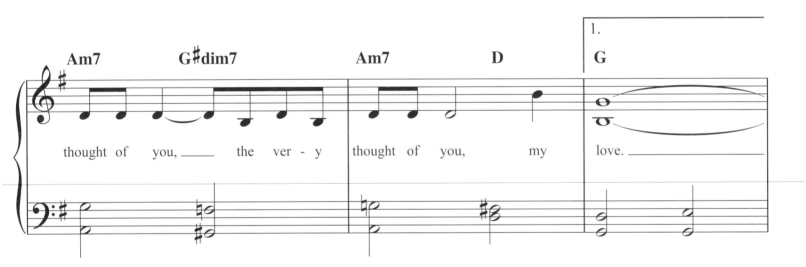

WILLOW WEEP FOR ME

Words and Music by
ANN RONELL

Wil-low weep for me, wil-low weep for me,

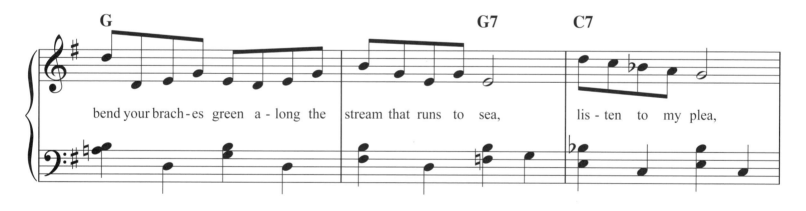

bend your brach-es green a-long the stream that runs to sea, lis-ten to my plea,

lis-ten, wil-low, and weep for me.

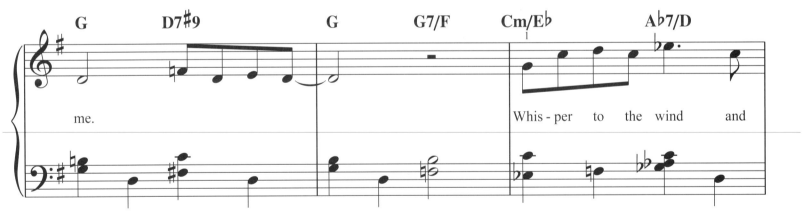

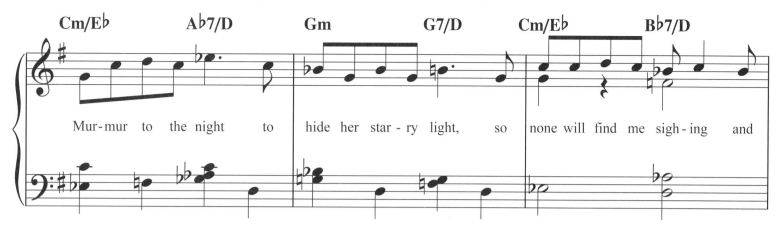

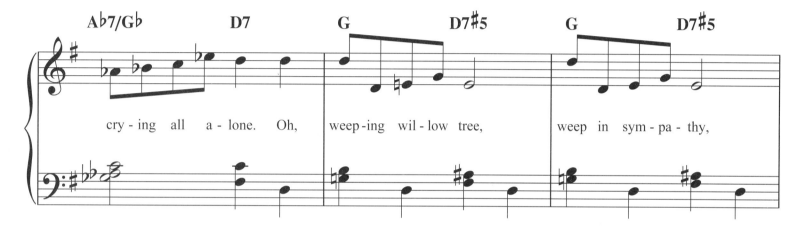

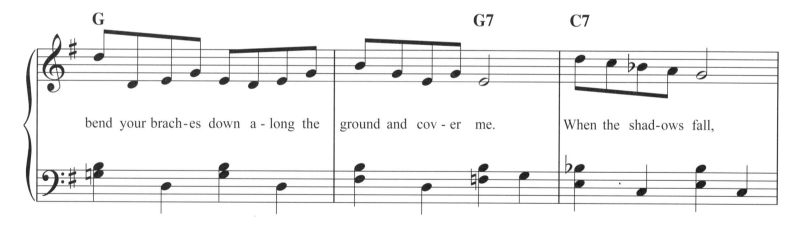

YARDBIRD SUITE

By CHARLIE PARKER

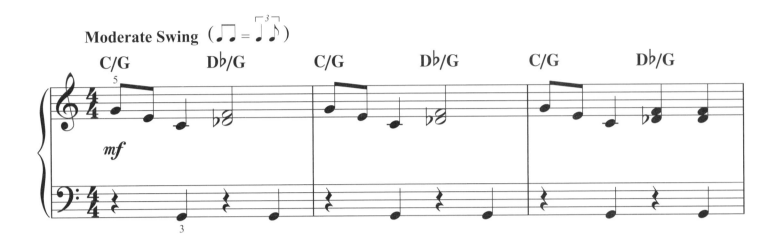

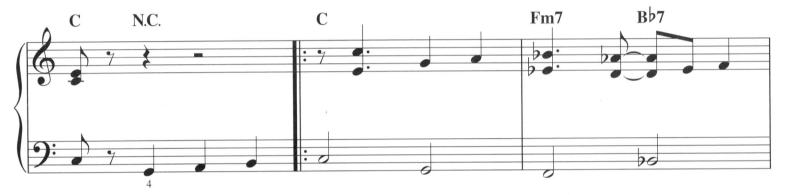

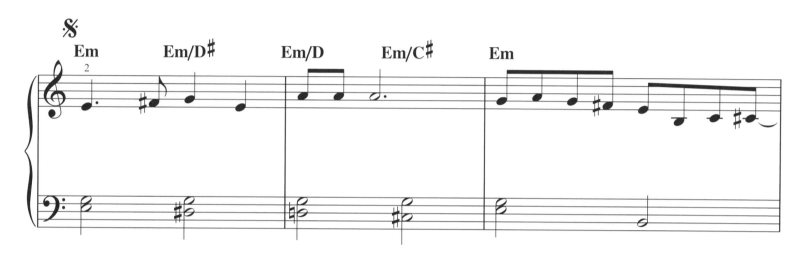

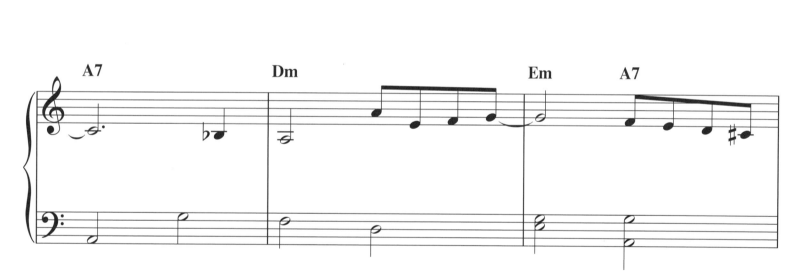

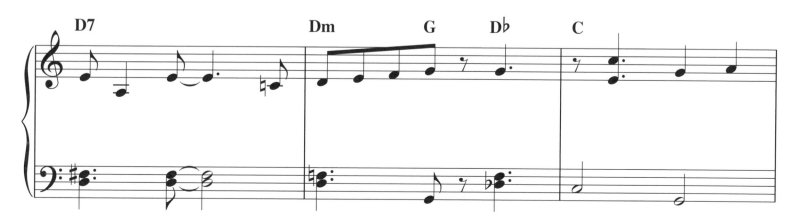

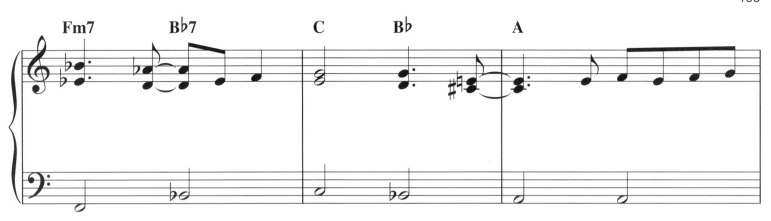

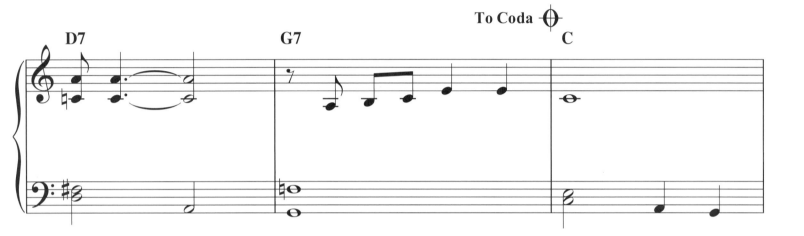

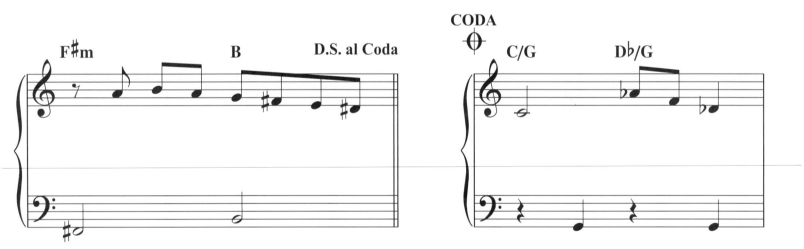

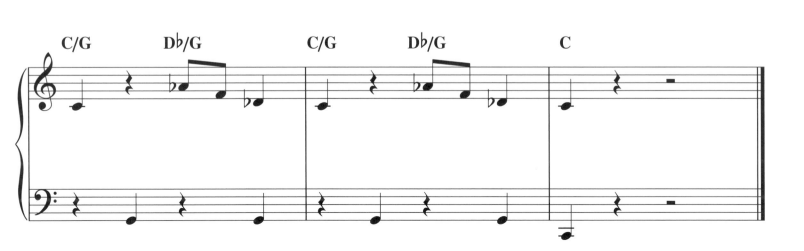

WITCHCRAFT

Music by CY COLEMAN
Lyrics by CAROLYN LEIGH

Moderately

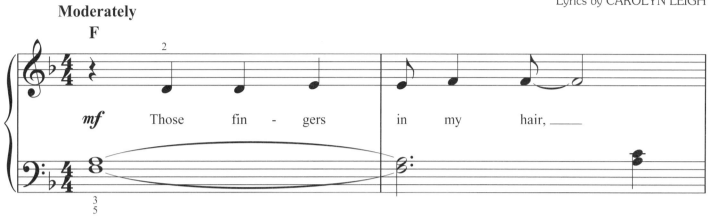

Those fin - gers in my hair, _____

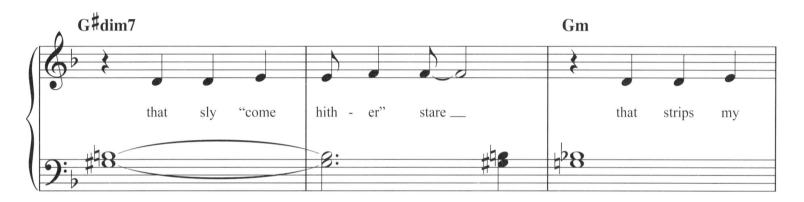

that sly "come hith - er" stare _____ that strips my

con - science bare, _____ it's witch - craft. _____

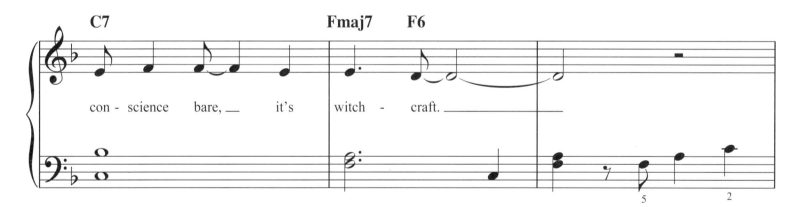

And I've got no de - fense _____ for it,

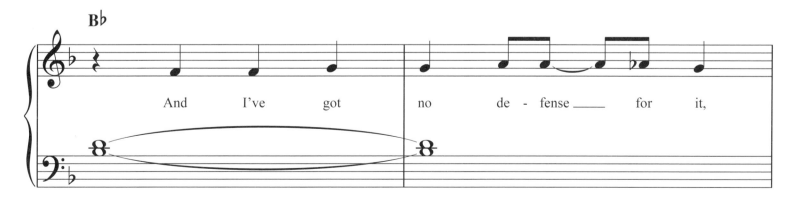

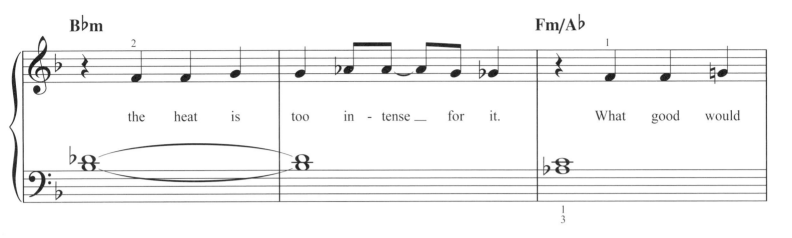

the heat is too in - tense ___ for it. What good would

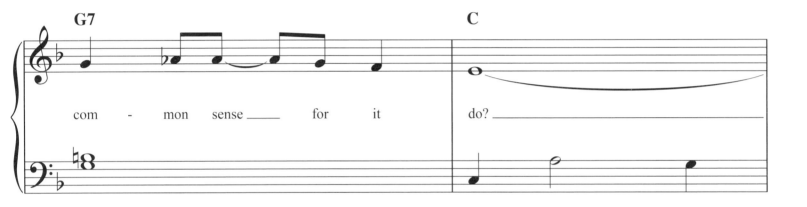

com - mon sense ___ for it do? _____

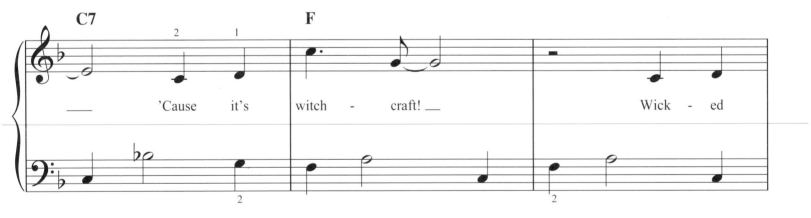

___ 'Cause it's witch - craft! ___ Wick - ed

witch - craft. ___ And al - though I know ___

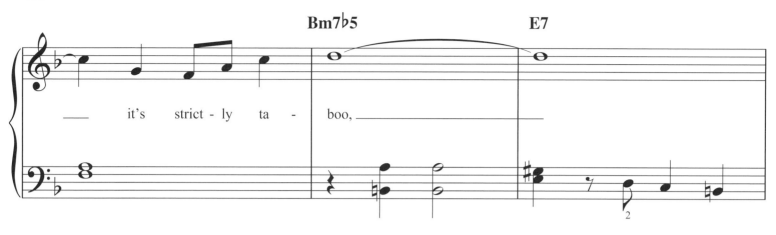

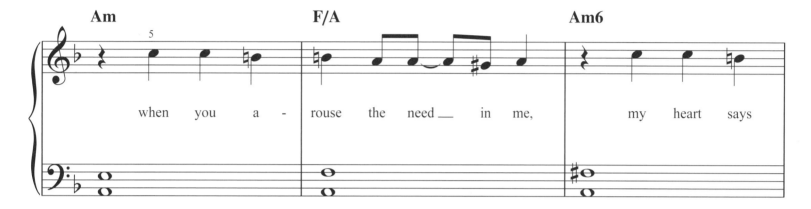

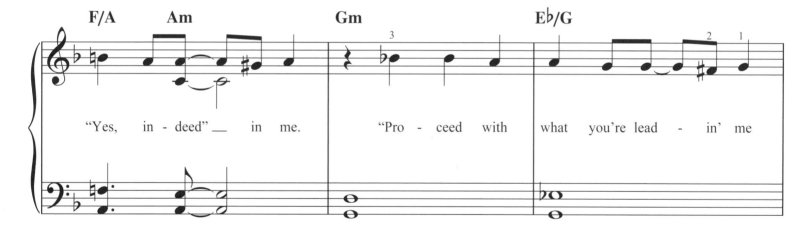

157

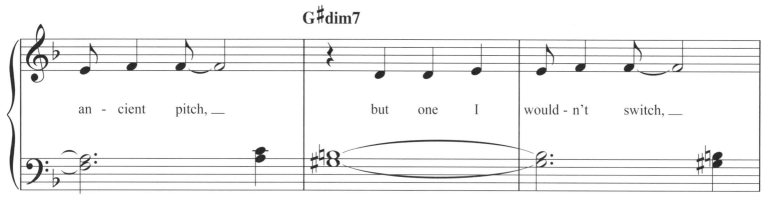

G#dim7

an - cient   pitch, ___   but   one   I   would - n't   switch, ___

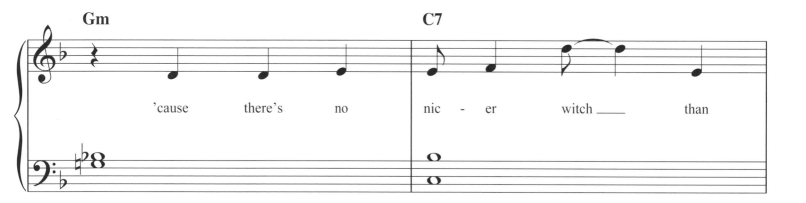

Gm   C7

'cause   there's   no   nic - er   witch ___   than

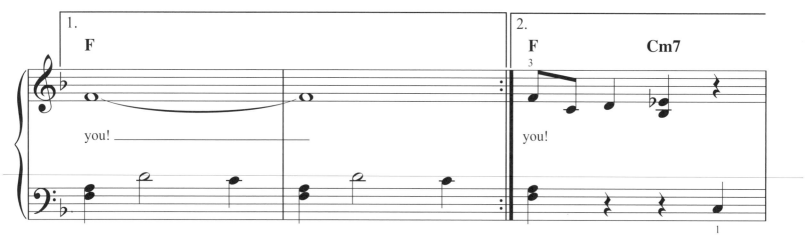

1.
F   2.
F   Cm7

you! ___   you!

F6   Cm7   F   G♭6   F6

YESTERDAYS

from ROBERTA

Words by OTTO HARBACH
Music by JEROME KERN

Moderately slow, in 2

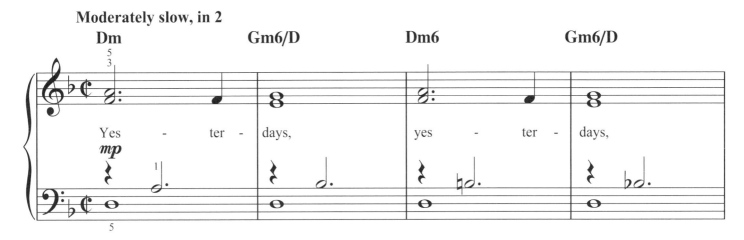

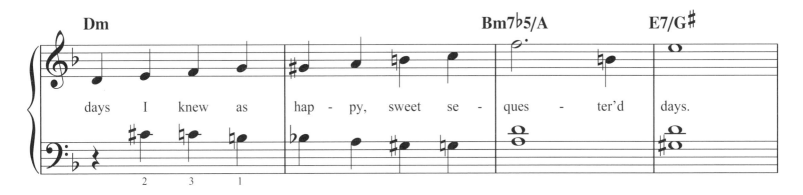

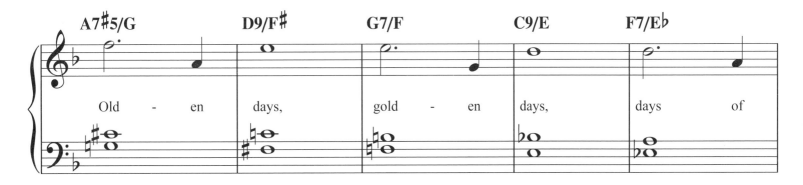

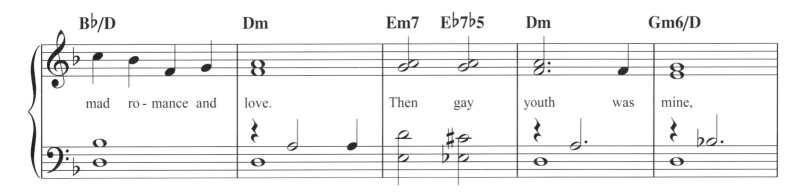

truth was mine, joy - ous free and flam - ing life, for -

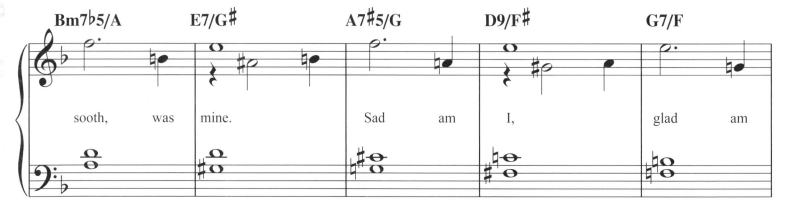

sooth, was mine. Sad am I, glad am

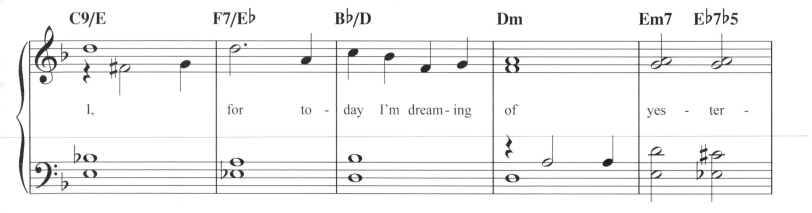

I, for to - day I'm dream - ing of yes - ter -

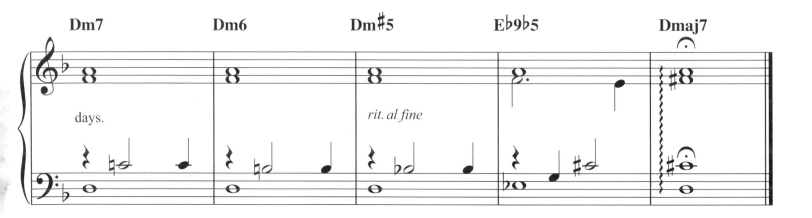

days. *rit. al fine*

FIRST 50 SONGS
YOU SHOULD PLAY ON THE PIANO

You've been taking lessons, you've got a few chords under your belt, and you're ready to buy a songbook.
*Now what? Hal Leonard has the answers in its **First 50** series.*

These books contain easy to intermediate arrangements with lyrics for must-know songs.
Each arrangement is simple and streamlined, yet still captures the essence of the tune.

3-Chord Songs
00249666..............................$17.99

4-Chord Songs
00249562..............................$17.99

Acoustic Songs
00293416..............................$17.99

Baroque Pieces
00291453..............................$15.99

Blues Songs
00293318..............................$15.99

Broadway Songs
00150167..............................$17.99

Christmas Carols
00147216..............................$15.99

Christmas Songs
00172041..............................$15.99

Classical Pieces
00131436..............................$15.99

Country Songs
00150166..............................$16.99

Disney Songs
00274938..............................$22.99

Duets
00276571..............................$19.99

Early Rock Songs
00160570..............................$15.99

Folk Songs
00235867..............................$15.99

Gospel Songs
00282526..............................$15.99

Hymns
00275199..............................$15.99

Jazz Standards
00196269..............................$15.99

Kids' Songs
00196071..............................$15.99

Latin Songs
00248747..............................$17.99

Movie Songs
00150165..............................$17.99

Movie Themes
00278368..............................$17.99

Pop Ballads
00248987..............................$17.99

Pop Hits
00234374..............................$17.99

Popular Songs
00131140..............................$17.99

R&B Songs
00196028..............................$17.99

Relaxing Songs
00327506 ....$17.99

Rock Songs
00195619..............................$17.99

Songs by the Beatles
00172236..............................$22.99

TV Themes
00294319..............................$15.99

Worship Songs
00287138..............................$19.99

HAL•LEONARD®

www.halleonard.com

Prices, content and availability subject to change without notice.